T0246388

THE WARRIOR POET WAY

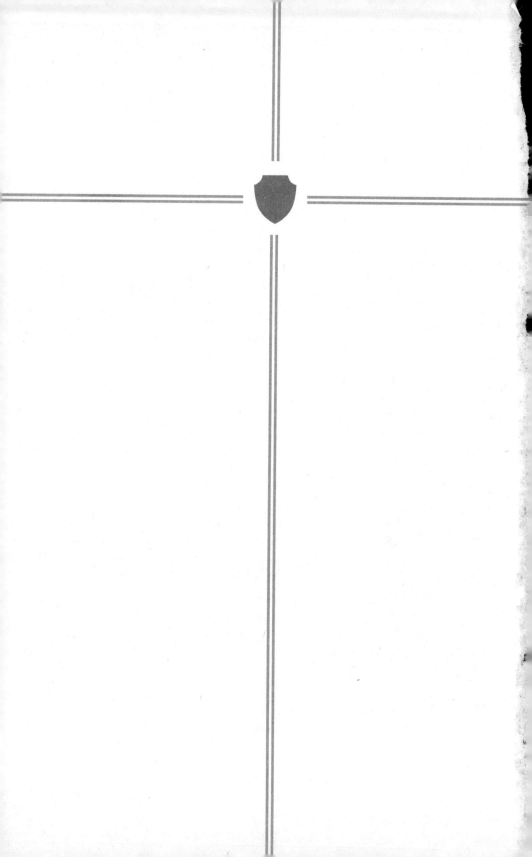

THE
WARRIOR
POET WAY

A GUIDE TO LIVING FREE
AND DYING WELL

JOHN LOVELL

SENTINEL

SENTINEL
An imprint of Penguin Random House LLC
penguinrandomhouse.com

Most Sentinel books are available at a discount when purchased in quantity for sales promotions or
corporate use. Special editions, which include personalized covers, excerpts, and corporate imprints,
can be created when purchased in large quantities. For more information, please call (212) 572-2232
or e-mail specialmarkets@penguinrandomhouse.com. Your local bookstore can also assist with
discounted bulk purchases using the Penguin Random House corporate Business-to-Business
program. For assistance in locating a participating retailer, e-mail B2B@penguinrandomhouse.com.

Library of Congress Cataloging-in-Publication Data
Names: Lovell, John (Veteran), author.
Title: The warrior poet way: a guide to living free and
dying well / John Lovell.
Description: [New York, NY] : Portfolio/Penguin, [2023]
Identifiers: LCCN 2023002448 (print) | LCCN 2023002449 (ebook) |
ISBN 9780593541845 (hardcover) | ISBN 9780593541852 (ebook)
Subjects: LCSH: Masculinity. | Calmness. | Protection.
Classification: LCC BF692.5 .L68 2023 (print) | LCC BF692.5 (ebook) |
DDC155.3/32—dc23/eng/20230501
LC record available at https://lccn.loc.gov/2023002448
LC ebook record available at https://lccn.loc.gov/2023002449

Printed in the United States of America
7th Printing

BOOK DESIGN BY ALISSA ROSE THEODOR

*This book is dedicated to the Warrior Poets of the past
who carried the torch through the ages. May our
brotherhood continue to follow in their
footsteps with courage and virtue.*

CONTENTS

INTRODUCTION

A FORGOTTEN BROTHERHOOD

All men dream: but not equally. Those who dream by night in the dusty recesses of their minds wake up in the day to find it was vanity, but the dreamers of the day are dangerous men, for they may act their dreams with open eyes, to make it possible.

—T. E. LAWRENCE

B ehind my house I have a shooting range, which occasionally becomes a battlefield.

Allow me to explain. When I "go shooting," I go to war. When all my targets are set up, all pieces of cover arranged, guns loaded, equipment checked, and my course of fire planned, I gear up into a hyperfocused battle calm.

Once I begin, after the first few shots have rung out and my heart starts pumping, the targets dissolve and in their place, I find *me*.

I suppose I get carried away, lost in the moment, and forget that this is just a shooting drill. Maybe my body remembers real combat and spurs me to move faster and use my angles of cover perfectly, as if my life depended on it. But in my head, the ghost I'm fighting is myself, just a little more skilled and only a moment away from killing me. I must be exact. I must move faster. I must get him first.

This ghost doesn't only find me on the gun range. He comes at me in my conscience. I'm visited by him at work, and in my home, haunted by the better man I am capable of becoming—and still am not.

Now before you call a shrink, understand I'm not actually seeing phantoms, nor am I wallowing in some damaged sense of shame and self-loathing. I simply recognize that no man is what he could be. We all could be more than we are; and if we were able to become that, imagine the compounding impact it would have on the world around us. Our sons would be raised stronger. Our wives would flourish. Our friends and neighbors would be impacted for the better. Everything would change.

Most men do their best while struggling to live up to an ever-changing list of responsibilities and obligations. And no matter what they have to offer, no matter how hard they strive, it's never enough. I know these taunts too well, plagued by my own potential: a man fully alive without the weights of fear, apathy, selfishness, procrastination, and insecurity. Deep down, I know I can be more, but often this gap between who I am and ought to be feels like too much to bridge.

The world keeps changing its definition of what a man is, and most of us are confused about this shifting target. It's easy to want to give up, to throw in the towel and simply choose to be less. But that doesn't work, either. Refusing to step up and lead in an increasingly chaotic and confusing world isn't the answer.

Underneath all these expectations, I believe there is something deep and true tugging at the heart of every man, something that keeps us up at night and wakes us early in the morning. It gnaws at our souls, taunting us with thoughts and images of what we might become. Maybe you feel it, too, this sacred call to your potential. I'm not talking about amping up your productivity or applying clever tricks from self-help books. I'm talking about actually *being* better. If the dormant parts of you and me came fully awake, imagine the lives that would benefit—those of our wives and children, as well as our coworkers and community members, even our friends. The impact could write a legacy for generations to come.

If you've ever considered this question of what you could be, your soul probably aches at the thought. It might seem all but impossible to achieve, because no matter how hard you try, you just can't seem to get it right. This sense of not-right-ness can bring with it feelings of shame and failure, and those never seem to go away. Such pressure can crush a man. But this is not where the story ends.

Men were meant for more. And yet, everywhere we look, we are being asked to be less. As society tempts us with pleasure, comfort, and security, we can be quietly lulled into passivity, giving up the fight for what we know to be right. We do this because it is easy—for now. Like the biblical Esau, we exchange our birthright for a temporary meal, surrendering the fight of our lives for something safe and predictable. And although we play nice, many men rage inside, knowing what fools we've been, settling for less than our true inheritance.

It is an ideal we are after.

Men want purpose, respect, and significance—something noble and worthy of their strength. But the world doesn't present us with a tidy package of what that ideal looks like, does it? How *should* I be, as a man in the world today? More sensitive and kind? Stronger and more stoic? Should I be a lover or a fighter? Is my aim to become a great war captain, like King Leonidas, or should I exchange the sword for a pen and model myself after Shakespeare? What makes a man great? His creative, romantic side; or his bold, sometimes reckless sense of daring? These are both noble ideals, but they are wildly different.

Or *are* they?

THE SEARCH FOR MORE

Years ago, I began a journey that seemed contradictory to many. I went from being a partying college frat boy to becoming a door-kicking Army Ranger. After that, though, I shifted careers into full-time Christian ministry and missions work, then as a gunfighting instructor, YouTuber, businessman, and public speaker. The changes continue, but my path wasn't just the varying jobs I've had. More than that, it's who I am—my own journey toward an impossible ideal.

On one hand, I wanted to be a more loving man. When I

returned to the civilian world after serving five tours in Ranger Battalion, I was seeking to become a better father, husband, and leader.

On the other hand, I was striving to become an even deadlier man, because I knew what dangers lurked out there, just beyond the comfort of our "civilized" world. I was aware of how vulnerable most people really are. I knew the cost of liberty and sought to be a better protector, provider, and defender of my freedom and that of others.

These seemingly contradictory pulls in my life were confusing, but I knew there was something true and paradoxical in my desire to be both dangerous and good.

From a young age, I had within me both a romantic poet and a savage warrior. For my part, there was no contradiction in these extremes and no need to compromise. I felt a deep connection to the great men of old but found little place for such ideals in present times. *Where were the cowboys and sages of today?* I wondered, *the great warriors and thinkers who weren't afraid to challenge the status quo?*

I wondered if maybe I was asking for too much. Had I spent too much time reading old books? Was I simply becoming an old man, pining for "the good old days"? Where had ancient masculinity gone, and was there any place for it in the modern world?

In almost every season of my life, I've felt like a square peg in a round hole. Although I belonged to different athletic teams, a college fraternity, an elite military unit, various friendship circles, and a dozen other clubs and organizations, something was always missing.

I wanted danger and adventure, a life of poetry and purpose that required waging war for what really mattered while celebrating the good things in life. I searched for other men who sought these same ideals, a true band of brothers, heroes ready to do battle—and wondered if I was alone.

I began to share my thoughts and ideas on YouTube as well as in the firearm training classes I was now leading, and men began to come out of the woodwork. Knowing they were capable of something greater than what society was telling them they could be, they wanted more as well.

As I shared my thoughts online and during our in-person classes, other men spoke up, sharing what resonated with them, and I saw that we were creating what we all had been yearning for. Over time, we organized ourselves into what we now call the Warrior Poet Society. To this day, I am flooded with daily testimonials and stories of how our movement has helped save marriages, safeguard warriors in times of danger, answer critical life questions, escape dead-end careers, and nourish more meaningful relationships.

It's been a wild ride.

What started with a few followers and some online rants grew to an audience of over a million people in just a few years. Today, our YouTube channel has well over one hundred million views and continues to grow through various media outlets. Our training company has also grown, and we are teaching thousands of people to defend themselves with guns, knives, and their bare hands.

More recently, we launched our own streaming service and app called WPSN (Warrior Poet Society Network) to provide people with anti-woke entertainment and news as well as full training courses and other programs for freedom-loving people.

This growing fraternity, however, is not just a group of protectors of liberty. We aren't playing war with our abundance of ammo and camo; we want more than a club. As men, we strive for something greater than we would otherwise be on our own. We are many, and at the same time, we are one. We know what we are capable of and won't accept anything less than our very best. We aim for an ideal that is still worth striving for.

We are Warrior Poets.

RISE OF THE WARRIOR POET

What is a Warrior Poet? Put simply, it is an antidote to a society that has forgotten what true masculinity is.

Today, our culture tends to celebrate victims over heroes. We praise weakness and a lack of discipline while villainizing aggression and strength. *Be passive*, we seem to tell men of all ages. *Go with the flow, be a nice guy, and do whatever the ruling class tells you.*

But shouldn't we be teaching our boys to trust their instincts and fight for what's right? Shouldn't young men everywhere be encouraged to question immoral authority and search for truth beyond what is socially acceptable? Should we not *expect* men to challenge evil, embrace what is good, and fight to protect it? In other words, shouldn't we be ready to rock the boat and stand unflinchingly against a world gone wrong?

There is still an ideal of what we can be. The goal of this book is to call you to that ideal.

To be a good man, you must become a paradox: strong but self-controlled, violent but gentle, ready to go to war one minute and prepared to give piggyback rides the next. This kind of man is fierce in word and deed while remaining compassionate and humble. He is fully soldier, fully lover, whole man.

This is what I call the Warrior Poet, and it is the standard required of all men. A whole man is not part Warrior and part Poet. He's all Warrior and all Poet. To be anything less than both is to be incomplete.

When a man goes to war, he doesn't take a part of himself, he takes the whole thing: body, mind, heart, and spirit. Any unconverted part can become an anchor dragging the Warrior down. Any uninitiated parts of a man will sabotage him in the strain of battle, resulting in deadly consequences. Just like how a chain can break at the weakest link, a man is only as strong as his greatest vulnerability.

Therefore, Warrior Poets train themselves in both the art of war as well as the daily challenges to live and love better. This kind of man loves a woman well and cares for his children. He goes off to battle when freedom is attacked and works tirelessly to provide for his family. His whole soul, body, and mind chase truth like a bloodhound. He wants to be at once awed by beauty and still deeply feel the tragedies of life.

This is what it means to be a whole man, to be a true Warrior Poet.

GOOD BUT DANGEROUS

You and I are called to a level of greatness that goes beyond personal legacy. We must be the unconquerable lion *and* the sacrificial lamb. The kind of man we will be exploring in this book is both committed to protecting the innocent as well as laying down his own life when required. He is good but dangerous.

The word "dangerous" is a concept our culture does not currently value when applied to men. The barrage of news headlines and propagandized attacks against masculinity has lulled the public into thinking there is only one kind of "dangerous"— the bad kind.

But there is an invisible liability in asking good men to suppress their warrior instincts: their longing for adventure, their natural boldness and strength. To dismiss what sets your soul on fire and live an existence that doesn't ruffle any feathers is not what you are here to do. It will not keep your loved ones safe, and it won't satisfy you.

Not to mention, it just doesn't work.

Battening down what makes you dangerous won't make your longings any quieter. It only adds fuel to the fire. A man who doesn't find a challenge worthy of his strength will find another outlet. He'll lose himself in sports teams, work, pornography, or going to the gym. He'll obsess over the next NFL game or some new video game or the next career goal, never quite satisfied with what's in front of him.

When left unchecked, our deepest desires will sabotage our most important relationships, coming out in passive-aggressive and often catastrophic ways. When men don't acknowledge their masculine nature, they are hurtling toward disaster, whether they realize it or not. A midlife crisis, moral failure—or more—are coming soon.

These men are the ones who, in the words of Henry David Thoreau, lead lives of "quiet desperation," wasting their strength and most important years. And I'm willing to bet that we have all been this man at least once or twice in our lives, wondering, *Is this as good as it gets?* and if there's more to being alive.

There is.

It's time we dug deep into our souls and answered that longing we all feel. It's time to become the kind of heroes the world needs but doesn't always want, to be what our families and communities deserve. It's time to step up and be what we always knew we were capable of.

LIVING FREE, DYING WELL

The Warrior Poet is a simple concept broad enough to encapsulate many kinds of men. I myself am a Christian, and this worldview influences everything I say and do, but we have many in our ranks who come from a broad base of ideologies. Still, we are united in our aim to be a living sacrifice for a cause greater than ourselves. That is our calling and burden: to live free and die well.

As broad as this mission is, it is impossibly difficult. Which is why we are always training, always striving to become better. If you can get behind that and are willing to put in the work, you are already one of us. We may differ on politics, theologies, and personal philosophies of life; but if you can rally around living for a higher purpose and sacrificing in defense of others, then this is your invitation to join us.

What does it mean to be part of the Warrior Poet Society?

It is more than a club. We are members of something sacred and ancient, a fraternity of men and women who love freedom and defend truth. We possess the mind of a student, the heart of a romantic, and the growing skills of a fighter.

Motivated by love, we are committed to defend others through becoming trained protectors. We are kind to the ones we love and fierce to those who deserve it. We are not lovers or fighters—we are both. After all, real love protects, and the best warriors love what they are fighting for and whom they are fighting to protect.

This is the kind of man we need more of today. He sees danger and wonder almost everywhere he looks, is willing to kill—and be killed—for what is right, and protects the vulnerable at all costs.

The question, then, is not: *Am I that kind of man?* Rather, the real question is: *How do I grow into being more of the man I already know I should be?*

A DARE TO BE DANGEROUS

This is a book about what it means to be a whole man. In the pages that follow, I've presented a path followed by both the great men who have come before us as well as those who are treading this journey with us today.

When we follow in these men's footsteps, we get closer to scratching the itch we all feel inside. How do we bring balance and significance to our lives? How do we love well and fight for what matters, facing our greatest fears and insecurities along the way?

Anyone can walk this path. You don't have to go to war, but conflict is inevitable. You don't have to fire a gun, but combat skills are useful—you will need to fight at some point, if only for what is true and good.

You don't have to adhere to any particular framework of belief, but you must believe in something bigger than yourself. It is not required to be a brilliant philosopher or high-minded intellectual, but you must love truth. You don't have to bench-press five hundred pounds, but strength will be necessary.

To answer this high calling will take work, and it won't always be easy. But I hope you do it anyway, because if not you, then who?

Not every man will read this, but you are. Let's start with us and what we know in our gut is possible. Someone needs to go first. Someone needs to say no to what is wrong with the world. To begin, it takes only an admission of where we fall short and a willingness to become better.

When I started this journey, I was discouraged by how hard it was to find an example of balance—a man both strong and kind, a killer *and* a lover. Since then, I've found many men and women who long for the same. This book is a documentation of the lessons I've learned from the men I now proudly call brothers. These are the ones who have already become legends and those who will become them in the future. And though I confess to not having mastered this balance, my goal is to encourage and challenge us onward and upward toward this standard. Let this book be a dare to you and me to aim higher than what others have expected or even required of us.

So let's talk about how this book works.

The Warrior Poet Way follows ten basic principles that have guided my understanding of what a real man is and ought to be. Starting with how to harness your own warrior spirit, then applying that strength to the rest of your life, we'll tackle one challenge at a time.

After that, we'll explore what it means to become "the most dangerous man in the room" as well as how to battle the inner coward that wants to ruin your life (and will, if you let him). We'll also talk about death and why we all must face it now so that we can be ready for it whenever it may come.

Then, we'll delve into what poets can teach us about love and life. I'll share what I learned from both the battlefield and the dance floor.

Through all this, I'll ask you to lean in to learn the secret of a successful life and the most important lessons I've learned about balance, romance, and discipline.

Finally, we'll talk about how to empower the next generation and practically safeguard our freedoms that are rapidly slipping away.

And because many of you, like me, love a challenge, each of these principles will contain a short practicum, which is just a fancy word for "something to do." I want this book to be more than an intellectual exercise. I want you to do something with it, so that by the end you have already started taking action, walking in the direction of becoming a better man.

The way has been set. All you have to do is decide where you stand. Are you one of us, ready to take on this great mantle? It won't be easy, but it will be worth it. This is our manifesto and duty. The road before us is neither safe nor comfortable, but it is beyond rewarding.

This is the Warrior Poet Way. Let's begin.

THE WARRIOR POET WAY

1

A World in Need of Warriors

Wars may be fought with weapons, but they are won by men. It is the spirit of men who follow and of the man who leads that gains the victory.

—GEORGE S. PATTON

The tension was unbearable. I tried to control my breathing as I looked out on where our battle would take place. This was the calm before the storm. My heart was already in my chest, my nerves on edge. Behind me was my compatriot, a brave artillery soldier serving as backup, a pile of hand grenades at the ready should things go south.

As my fellow soldier lurked behind the cover of our newly made fortification, before me a head peeked out from behind a tree. We were surrounded by the elements with only our wits and our courage to aid us. My eyes met those of my opponent. Though the outcome of the fight was uncertain, I knew that today was not my day to die. Other soldiers had seen such insuperable odds and had not been so fortunate. Nonetheless, battle called, and I had to answer.

It was time.

My enemy sauntered out with a bo staff—that is, a stick he found in the backyard. *Not as good as mine*, I thought with a sneer. We came together, meeting on the field of combat, immediately engaging each other, staff hitting staff. We stood there as fearless children-at-arms doing battle while mortars exploded around in all directions.

That day, we suffered significant losses while accomplishing great feats, surviving to live yet another day. Thank God.

When the battle concluded, we retreated to our separate barracks, and our commanding officers bestowed the coveted ice-cream sandwiches on us as worthy war trophies.

I was only eight years old, playing with my neighbors and siblings in the woods; but it was then that I knew the sweet taste of victory. It tasted like vanilla.

BORN INTO BATTLE

Those little neighborhood battles are cherished memories from my childhood. My parents didn't teach us to play war in the woods, but without any instruction whatsoever, we managed to forge our own weapons and compete in combat every summer. It was instinct—and that is quite telling, isn't it?

At an early age, boys understand that there are bad guys in

the world who must be stopped. In their minds, mostly every-thing is a competition, each and every moment translated into a who-would-win scenario. My own children used to endlessly pit animals and heroes against each other in hypothetical skirmishes and discuss the potential outcomes. *Would a tiger beat a lion?* They'd even read books on these subjects to figure out the answer.

As they've grown and are now learning more history, they're seeing the strength of both the hero and foe in real-life battles and what made the tides turn. The Warrior Within is awaken-ing in them. They recognize that a battle is being waged, and that something is required of them. Every man does.

We have known it since we were young, imagining our-selves as knights and army men, fighting monsters. This is why every stick, toy, or vegetable became an instant weapon for many of us while growing up. Nobody told us to play this way. We came by it naturally.

Before they're out of diapers, boys are preparing for battle. This is a natural and normal impulse. If you give both a boy and a girl a Barbie doll, you would not be surprised to see the girl dressing the doll in pretty clothes and playing princess. The boy, on the other hand, will hold the legs in one hand, push the upper body back at a 90-degree angle and pretend the Barbie is a gun. Then, he'll point the gun at someone and shoot. An hour later, the doll will be missing a leg with the head turned around back-ward. Sure, there are exceptions to the rule, but I'm not talking about outliers. I'm talking about the rule of what's at the heart of true masculinity, which is to protect and defend.

Many parents might be tempted to stop this kind of play, to interfere with the boy's impulses, but that would be unwise. Of course, you can let the child know it's not good to pop the heads off his sister's toys, but be careful to not chastise the aggression out of a young male.

Instead, it must be controlled and channeled—but never eliminated. He and his future family and community may need his aggression someday. Any child who has done something like this is answering an ancient call to the ranks of previous generations who came before, every generation of men who made the next possible, each understanding the same intuitive truth: *We are at war.*

And wars require warriors.

MAKING ROOM FOR MEN

Do you remember when you would see heroes on TV and in movies, and they *stood* for something? Remember John Wayne, Clint Eastwood, Sean Connery? Remember, even, the next-door neighbor who came over when they noticed that your power was out?

There was a time not too long ago when men were allowed to be strong. Of course, these men were far from perfect, but we understood what they were and what they could be. It was not uncommon to see them open a door for a lady or pull over to help someone change a tire. We knew the meaning of masculinity, and at the heart of it was sacrifice.

It seems today we've lost this understanding; the importance of having warriors in the world. Sure, we still see superheroes in comic books and movies, as well as occasional astronauts and cowboys as objects of respect and reverence. But this is far different from growing up with Buzz Aldrin and Neil Armstrong. Where are the *real* men today who possess rugged strength and who commit to bold action? When did we start expecting so little?

Maybe this kind of man seems mythological at best, but I assure you that such men still exist. There are men who will still stand up for what is right and who aren't afraid to use their strength. We used to require this of them; now it surprises us. If we want to have any hope for the future, though, we must return to such an expectation.

We must summon the part of us that our society hasn't completely squashed with the hammer of political correctness. We've been lulled into pursuing our "sensitive" side so much that it has become, for many men, their *only* side. Men need to wake up to their true identities as warriors. This is the only way we win in any fight. Yes, a man needs to know when to be gentle, but gentleness alone will not keep tyranny and evil at bay. It's going to take warriors to defend what we've built and hold dear.

Consider this, then, your invitation to ignore the seething, postmodern feminist shrieking against the patriarchy. It's okay to *want* to be a warrior. Although mutilating dolls is not what we want our sons to do, the idea of being a warrior who can one day offer loving protection to the innocent is an instinct we should protect.

Some mothers may be shocked to see their boys playing war

games at a very young age, but it is good. Whether encouraged or not, most will happen upon them, regardless; and when a boy starts playing war, he is learning something essential about his nature. To fight for the freedom of others is a noble act that should be encouraged. Even if the fight is pretend, the courage is real.

Boys love a fight. They inherently understand that one day they will be protectors of others, and at a certain age it becomes natural to answer such a call. You'll see them putting it together in their own haphazard way, seeking greater opportunities for responsibility, risk, and independence. Young men are always searching for ways to test their strength. My sons plan surprise attacks on me, pouncing as soon as I walk through the front door. They want to see if they have what it takes, continually testing themselves, using their dad as a measuring stick. Instinctively, they are preparing to become the bedrock of strength upon which society is built.

One day, my boys will be the strong arm that freedom rests on, and all these exercises will have hopefully prepared them.

REMEMBERING WHAT YOU ARE

While a boy may know he should prepare for war, it is the adult who forgets. Remember what life was like as a child? It was serious *and* playful. There was always a war to wage, an enemy to overcome, something innocent to protect. As children, we *battled*. We made forts with barricades and reinforcements, issued passwords to ensure no one was able to enter our area unchallenged, especially the neighborhood dogs, and found a way to turn anything into a skirmish with high stakes. We looked for adventure every single day and found it. We defended what we held dear. The Warrior Within was always present.

As men, the impulse to wage war is still programmed into us. When we're kids, we explore trails and create castles in the sand naturally, subduing the wild around us. But as we get older, we don't quite know how this translates to real, adult life.

As a result, many men lose themselves in video games. These escapes offer an exploration of unknown worlds in their own way, involving the seeking of treasures and battling of foes in epic fights against evil. The warrior impulse is always there, showing up in surprising ways. We've only traded the real for the virtual, but the impulse remains.

Even in courting a girl, men are answering a sacred call to pursue. They do all kinds of audacious, stupid things for a beautiful woman. They chase her, give her gifts, sacrifice everything for one more shot at getting a chance to see her. Any guy who's been in love knows the fear and thrill of it—the electrifying first touch, the sheer horror of potential rejection, the sweat on his skin and fire in his veins. It's an adventure. Man lives to hunt, and she is his greatest pursuit. The problem occurs when many men forget the pursuit. They take for granted the beauty they've rescued—not because of her, but because they lost the will to hunt.

A man can never stop never stop hunting; it's in his DNA. Everything is a pursuit, a life-and-death scenario that requires his strength and courage. There is always a chase, either real or vicarious, and the stakes are always incredibly high. We were handcrafted for this adventure, and we will find it wherever we can.

Sadly, most men don't have an outlet for this. They watch football or soccer, instead, and roar at the TV screen as they see other men engaging in "battle." They cheer when the good guys destroy the Death Star or their political party trounces its opponent. It's exciting to watch, but none of it is the same as doing it yourself. At the deepest level, every man wants in on the action. Too often, though, he settles for a front-row seat to someone else's battle.

As long as a man trades his warrior instinct for entertainment, his soul will not be satisfied. He will be perpetually bored, searching for a way to kill time and quell his longings. A man who's consumed by his mission, however, who knows what life is about and his part to play, doesn't need a distraction. His life *is* the adventure.

SUMMON THE WARRIOR WITHIN

I teach gunfighting for a living. Literally. Like, that's my job. I travel the country and instruct others on tactical rifle and concealed carry pistol training, room clearing, small-unit tactics, low-light fighting, home defense, and other skills. "Firearms instructor" isn't the right title. I'm not just training marksmanship; I'm teaching people to use the right tools and skills to defeat the greatest apex predator the world has ever known: *man.*

This is no small feat. Being a strong man capable of hurting people is not enough to defeat this incredible adversary. We have to learn to work with ourselves and train our own warrior spirit, coaxing him back to life in a society where he has been lulled to sleep.

In the Warrior Poet Society Pistol 3 class, I run our students through an unnerving exercise. The point is to introduce them to the stress of a real gunfight. The first thing we do is have them put on protective gear, then convert their guns to shoot training munitions that won't kill but sure do sting. Next, we place two students across from each other and have them extend their arms so that only their fingertips are touching. Their guns are at their sides, ready for my command.

Then, I have them wait. And wait. I leave them in that moment for a while to just breathe through the stress of the scenario. I let them look into each other's eyes and allow the fear to wash over them. This is stress-inoculation training at its finest, and it is a riot to watch firsthand.

What I want them to do is sit in that horrible moment, the calm before the storm, and look at each other, waiting. In this moment is a lesson: all you have is right here and there's no telling what comes next. A man who learns to control his fears and impulses and focus on the moment is a man who has learned to love life.

Finally, I give them the command: "FIGHT!" Then all hell breaks loose. The soldiers break into battle. One may try to try to disarm the other, or they might both stand their ground and shoot it out like an old-fashioned Western. There is always shooting, moving, laughing, and some mild bleeding.

What you often see is guys coming up with something they think is a great idea and just get toasted as their best-laid plan completely crumbles before their eyes. Then, they walk away, laughing, realizing how stupid their idea was. After that, we get them back into another fight so they can try again. They are initiates now, and more training will soon follow.

These men have awakened their Warrior Within and are now flooded with ideas and instincts that only moments before were dormant. For the rest of the training, they'll test all kinds of theories to see what works and learn from their mistakes.

The point of the exercise is to teach our students who the real enemy is. It's not the man they're staring at; he's only the target. The biggest opponent in any situation is you. At this point, these guys have been trained to properly draw a gun, establish a grip, press a trigger, do emergency reloads, and so on. They know the skills and drills, but fear alone can cause them to clumsily paw at their guns, missing the opportunity to draw and fire. Stress shuts down an unpracticed warrior, causing him to lock up, rendering him immobile. This is true for anyone, and the way to overcome this resistance is only through practice. And as the day continues, these men get the training they need. They do the drill over and over again until they have quieted the voices of fear and summoned something stronger and more primal. It turns out that we don't have to *find* the Warrior Within. He's been there since childhood. What we have to do is train him.

A WORLD AT WAR

The world is not a safe place. According to the historian Will Durant, in the past 3,421 years there have been only 268 years entirely free of conflict, which is less than 8 percent of all recorded human history. Reality is not the haven of rainbows and butterflies we'd like to believe. It is a little less Disney and a lot more Brothers Grimm than we've been taught or told. There are real villains out there, it turns out, and it's going to take more than niceties to stop them.

A man needs to trudge the ancient paths of true masculinity. We must return to our timeless roles as protectors, providers, leaders, and caretakers of all we have been entrusted with. How do we begin, though? Where do we start in reclaiming our birthright? In a word: *courage.*

Courage is still contagious. All we need is someone, anyone, to go first. That's you. That's me. That's all of us. When I talk about a *society* of Warrior Poets, this is what I'm talking about: men willing to run into the heat of conflict in defense of what is good. We have examples of men in the world doing just that, modeling what we are capable of. I am still moved by the stories of patriots and heroes going into the throes of battle and overcoming impossible odds for the sake of something bigger than themselves. These men inspire me and challenge me to stand up for what's right, even when it costs me something. Courage has not disappeared. It's merely been hibernating, waiting to be awakened. And the time is now.

Please don't misunderstand and think I'm asking you to don MultiCam uniforms and grab a rifle to go into a literal war. I mean much of this metaphorically, as we are in a fight for our values, traditions, and the right to create the free and fulfilled life we desire. There is also a war of ideas that will require us to be courageous with our words and decisions. And there is yet another battle about how we go about making an honest living while so many dishonest shortcuts are within arm's reach.

Yes, there is also a war of physical violence that may come calling in an instant, and if you aren't ready for it, your family could pay the price for your inability to protect them. Most of us haven't seen this threat materialize, and many never will. But it happens every day around us; and it is our sacred duty to be ready, not just apathetically play the odds. So the war surrounds us in various forms, and it is our job to respond in whatever way is required. One way or another, we will have to fight.

Every day, I see courageous men looking for an outlet for all this energy they have. Hidden in them is a yearning for personal responsibility and unbounded strength and humility. Young men especially are yearning for an occasion to test themselves, a challenge that forces them to bring their best selves forward.

This desire, I believe, is buried deep in the souls of all men and is something that cannot be eradicated. It can be hidden, pushed down deep, but never destroyed. It is who we are. Freedom is not what most men have known throughout history, and to maintain what we have, we are going to have to fight—to push back against the dangers of life and evils of the world.

And who will do this? Certainly not a nice, compliant man. We need men who will fight for truth in a world of lies and defend the cause of freedom where tyranny would otherwise reign. Only a warrior can do that.

What, exactly, *is* a warrior? A warrior is someone who is good at winning a fight and bad at being killed. A warrior may fight for all kinds of reasons, but it takes a man of violence to stop the threat of violence. To earn the privilege of our freedom, we need warriors to do the job.

Will that be you?

WHAT WILL YOU FIGHT FOR?

As we have seen, most every boy loves a good fight, and this desire is alive in virtually every man. It's just been domesticated out of many of us. We still, however, find occasion to fight: through playing sports, watching violent movies, and even trying to overcome our competitors in business. Admit it: you love to fight when you are on the winning side. Who doesn't like the feeling of hard-won victory?

The question is, what are you fighting *for*?

G. K. Chesterton wrote, "A true warrior fights not because he hates what is in front of him, but because he loves what is behind him." Good men do not fight because they love to kill; they fight because they have something worth protecting. A soldier will lay down his life for the cause of freedom, if he believes in it, so that others can choose the kind of life they want.

There will always be people who want to take away your liberties. Men who obtain power will try to keep that power, even if it means subduing others by means of manipulation, deceit, or brute force. Tyranny looks different now than it did centuries ago; much of the oppression we experience today is subtle, sneaking into our lives through compromise. It's the proverbial frog slowly being boiled to death. How do you destroy a man's freedom? By slowly taking away his ability to choose. Make no mistake, though: What follows political oppression is inevitably brute force. We must be ready.

It's not just physical violence we should fear, but also something deeper and more pernicious. Every day, we are fed marketing messages via our screens, coaxed into political correctness due to the influence of mainstream media, and cleverly coerced into a worldview that is not our own. We are told what and how to think, even what we can and cannot say, risking being "canceled" and other consequences if we speak our minds too freely. George Orwell was right when in *1984* he said, "But if thought corrupts language, language can also corrupt thought." When they win the battle of the mind, every other victory is imminent.

What we need to stand against these forces is a warrior. The modern warrior does not just fight against physical threats but also stands in opposition to destructive philosophies and foolish arguments. These men can be lawyers, public speakers, politicians, business owners, tradesmen, social media influencers, teachers, police officers, pastors, and hundreds of others professions. They are all on the front lines to fight against freedom-destroying ideologies. We must join them.

We cannot accept the way things are simply because we are told to. We must reclaim the warriors we have always been, so that when the fight comes, we are ready. If the war of ideas gives way to physical force, as it often does, we must be ready to do our part. As Thomas Jefferson said, "The tree of liberty must be refreshed from time to time with the blood of patriots and tyrants."

SMART OR STRONG?

Not long ago, my family and I were out to dinner one night, and I asked my older son a question. John Lucas was seven years old at the time and missing one of his front teeth. A generally happy child, his greatest worry in the world was what kind of LEGO set he would build next. In many respects, he was the dictionary definition of innocence.

"Son," I said, "which is better: to be smart or strong?"

I was in the mood to argue in favor of being smart, hoping to drum up an opportunity to lead my kids into realizing how important education, reading, and creativity are. But as John Lucas was deep in thought, my younger son, Judah, sensing my leading, blurted out, "Being smart! Being smart is more important!"

Before I could respond, John Lucas said, "Strong!"

"Why?" I asked.

"Because," he said, "if you were strong, you could beat up bad guys easier."

Then I looked back at Judah to see why he had said "smart," expecting him to say something about how you could do better at life or something. "If you are smart," he answered, "you could figure out a way to get *behind* the bad guy and beat him."

I roared with laughter.

We weren't talking about fighting or defending or anything of the sort. Fighting is a far less common subject in our house than reading classic books or building forts. My boys aren't into guns yet except for the occasional Nerf fight or BB gun. One day soon, we will walk that path together—but not today. What I found most interesting about the way the boys answered my question is they both filtered it through the lens of "Which would help me defeat a bad guy?" Quite telling, isn't it?

In Ranger Battalion, it's a long-running joke that there are only two types of Rangers: smart ones and strong ones. Sure, there's everyone in between, but most men lean toward one extreme or the other. Think, "Hulk, smash!" versus Captain America. Nobody wants to be the big dumb guy when you can be the brave hero. This is a joke, because it's a clever way of telling your buddy that you think he's stupid. The strong Ranger thinks you're complimenting him when really you're calling him an idiot. (Don't ever call a Ranger "dumb," or he might Hulk smash you—and you will have earned it.)

The truth is that we need both our strength and our smarts. The strong warrior has learned to direct his forcefulness at a target and eradicate. But he is also incomplete. Why? Because he has not yet become a smart warrior, a man who knows how to deal with his emotions instead of letting them run roughshod over his life. To win the fight of our lives, though, we have to be both smart and strong.

THE POWER OF ANGER

Strong warriors summon their rage to win a fight, but they don't know what to do when an immediate threat is not in front of them. These warriors often feel afraid. They channel their fear into anger and then use that anger to spring into action, attacking the enemy like Wolverine. I've seen it enough times to know that these men are onto something. There's no doubt about it: warriors get the job done.

The obvious problem, though, is when the conflict is over and the next challenge is not winning the war but winning at life. When this happens, all these men know is how to be mad. The Hulk was amazing in times of battle but had little chance of settling down with the beautiful Natasha Romanoff. She demanded another kind of warrior. Most women do.

On the other hand, the calculating warrior—the one who will not be ruled by his anger—still has all that rage at his disposal but finds a way to control it. Regardless of the chaos happening around him, he can maintain incredible focus and clear thinking, then employ violence when needed. When I observed men like this in Ranger Battalion, the common denominator I observed among them was control. They not only had the greater chance of winning a fight but also of living a balanced life. A Warrior Poet is a man who is balanced and controlled, clear about his mission and the tools he has at his disposal. He may feel fear or even get angry, but he doesn't let his feelings drive his life. He also doesn't try to wish them away with niceness; he allows himself to be angry and violent but always does so from a place of self-control.

Now, I wish I could say that every Ranger is balanced in the ways that I appreciate "balance," but the truth is that most members of the special operations community end up getting divorced. Oftentimes, they make poor life choices even if they are fantastic tacticians. My journey during and after Ranger Battalion set me on the Warrior Poet Way, which was driven by a desire to be a smart Ranger as well as a strong one—an angry one, as well as a calculating one.

Like the Hulk, many men are mad all the time and have no idea why. Maybe they weren't raised well or something happened when they were young. Perhaps they were betrayed one too many times or constantly feel that the world is against them. In their misery, they rage; and this kind of uncontrolled anger is dangerous for everyone.

Beware being the angry guy.

Ever seen a UFC fighter lose their cool in the octagon? They either immediately win or lose, and it's much more likely that they go down hard. Even to a fighter, anger is a fickle tool to employ. In a sudden flurry, it may gain you a quick victory, but in a longer entanglement, it will be strangled out by despair, broken heartedness, or another soul invader.

If your power is drawn from anger, then the only way to keep your strength is to keep getting angrier. You might win a few fights, but ultimately it will destroy you. There's just no way that ends well. It is good to be capable of violence, but God help us if we aren't controlled.

There is a fatal difference in controlling your anger versus your anger controlling you. For example, I am angry at the terrorist trying to kill the innocent—that is a fact. But when anger consumes me, I have already lost a more important battle. If I calmly plot to overthrow the bad guy, similar to how a scientist might approach a problem, then I am able to grit my teeth and in the next moment fall like a thunderbolt.

To be a Warrior Poet is to be a shape-shifter: a lion in one moment, a lamb the next. Such flexibility allows us to function well in everyday life and excel at defending what we love. We may visit extremes, but we live in the balance.

DON'T BRING THE WAR HOME

I don't mean to say you shouldn't be the romantic, sensitive, funny guy. Much of life calls for this. Nobody wants their dad or husband or boss to be a stern, harsh stoic all the time. But life does not call for *only* these characteristics in men; we also want and need men to be strong and aggressive.

If you want to be a good husband, you will need measures of

both softness and strength. Love requires the greatest amount of daily courage, and we are consistently called to the pain of denying ourselves for the sake of another.

Personally, I want to be emotionally vulnerable to my wife, kids, closest friends, and family members. I need to be able to empathize with my neighbors, coworkers, and community members, to be kind and gentle when life calls for it. But I also recognize there is something more to masculinity than these attributes.

We should not be lovers or fighters; we should be both. To be all one thing at the expense of the other is to be deficient even in the one. To be a good lover, you must make steps to be a good fighter, and vice versa. Love protects and nurtures. If momma bear cannot protect her cubs, she may not be a momma for long.

So, a man must be a warrior, yes, but this does not make him a danger to those in his care. My wife wouldn't think twice about giving me a piece of her mind even when I'm dressed in full Ranger kit with blasters in hand (which I do, on occasion, just to spice things up). She understands what I am capable of, but I am gentle with her; and she knows nothing will change that.

Neither do my kids fear violence from me. I am not the angry war veteran who projects all his unresolved violence onto his kids. They're just boys, and I am first and foremost their dad. But I still teach my kids to fight. We embrace the warrior spirit in our home and have fun with it. At any given moment, my little minions may attack with legendary ferocity.

When my sons and I do battle, it is a clash of champions, a

battle royale. My seven-year-old likes to get a running start to initiate his attacks, and just before his formidable attack he pauses to scream a quote from Pumbaa the Warthog: "They CALL ME . . . Mr. Pig!" Following the war cry, he throws himself into a full sprint toward me and roars, "AHHHHHHH!"

This assault cry does not cease until the boy has hit me full force with every ounce of his forty-pound frame. He holds nothing back. He doesn't guard himself against any mighty blow I may throw at the last moment. Nothing is reserved. He has been entirely consumed by the heat of the attack and strikes as if he has nothing to lose. Frequently, during his many onslaughts, my son will pause to reveal an ear-to-ear smile. For him—and me— it's a game. He's playing for keeps, but he is having fun and enjoying every moment of it.

If you have never wrestled your kid, there is nothing as fun and bonding as a contest with your own child. I relish these experiences and wouldn't trade them for the world. My kids love nothing more than attacking their dad, and seeing what they can pull off. It's fun for me, too, but I also recognize something deep happening in this exchange. They are learning their own strength and how to emulate mine.

My nine-year-old no longer relies on brute force alone in his attacks. He has adopted cunning into his onslaughts, understanding the need for a soldier to be both smart and strong. My boy circles behind and waits for a moment's distraction before he leaps off furniture and headlocks me. Again, he is fearless. And he is just a boy, having ferocious fun with his dad. But he is also learning valuable skills within the confines of love and security. Home must be a place of safety, even when playing war.

Defending your family is a loving thing to do, but it does not work if you succeed at making everyone afraid of you, including those you claim to protect. You are not a freedom fighter in this case; you're just a brawler. I've seen too many dudes get deployed to war and do well in defending their countries but fail to switch gears back home. As a result, their relationships fail, they struggle to keep a job, and they are unhappy. They succeeded at war only to suck at life. A Warrior Poet wants more.

BALANCE IS THE IDEAL

In the film *Braveheart*, William Wallace fights against injustice with his heart, mind, soul, and strength. We see in his life a model that applies to us all. But his story, like that of many warriors, does not begin with a battle. It starts with a boy with a broken heart—with a loss of innocence.

Before he can stage a revolt against his enemy, the young Wallace must first leave home and get an education under the tutelage of his wise uncle. Years later, Wallace returns having learned art, poetry, and multiple foreign languages. He has also learned to read, which is no small thing for a peasant in medieval Europe. And yes, he's learned to fight. The boy matures into a mighty man, one who eventually threatens the power of kings and nobles alike. He can go toe to toe with the smartest of them and conquer almost any man in battle. He abhors lies but still considers himself a savage. In the words of Walt Whitman, he contains multitudes.

Wallace's story ends in sacrifice; he gives up his life for the sake of his country. At the end of the film, he is tempted to take a tranquilizer to numb the pain before his public execution but refuses. He does not want to lose his wits and say something that might betray his cause. He resists comfort, defies politicking and propriety, and faces injustice head-on. This is a man who won't comply with society's standards, one who believes in something greater than the status quo. He is a contradiction in the best sense.

This is our ideal: a man who is dangerous enough to kill and just might, but who is never out of control—a sacrificial savage. Such a man loves well and fights well, able to discern what is needed.

To hold these two seemingly polar opposites seems contradictory to many, but this is what true masculinity is and has always been. We must be radically safe for those under our care and protection, strong and gentle. Balanced.

DO NOT FORGET THE FIGHT

If you are reading this, you probably have much to take for granted. In the United States of America, we are protected by an incredible military and some of the most sophisticated technology in the world. We have the firepower to literally wipe out all human life on the planet. Because of this, and only because of this, we forget that there are still terrible enemies in the world. We pretend from our high tower that the world is a safe place. We may imagine our greatest threats to be "hate speech" or social inequities, but these are not the only battles we face. There are regimes that would not hesitate to slaughter my family in their sleep, if only they had the chance, and I try to not forget this.

I hope you won't, either.

In the Twin Towers attack of September 11, 2001, nearly three thousand innocent civilians who were going about their daily lives were murdered. Sadly, terrorist attacks are not so shocking anymore. It no longer bewilders me to hear of another cowardly assault by one faction or another. Of course, I hate to hear about these things; I rage and mourn over such attacks, but they are far from surprising.

So what do we do? We must become the warriors we already know ourselves to be. When the world would have you be silent and harmless, do the opposite. Stand up and summon your boldness, tap into the innate wildness buried deep within your soul. Engage in the war of ideas. Speak the truth and do not self-censor your speech in fear. Live as if you are free, and you will be.

Learn to control your aggression. Become better than the Hulk and train your inner warrior. Be the man your family and country require. Do this now while you still can. Though you may not receive the respect you deserve, you are our only hope. As you learn to reconnect with and revitalize your strength, remember to temper it, pointing it toward the greatest challenges the world throws at you.

The world needs warriors. It is, however, best cared for by men who can thrive in eras of peace and war, who can willingly turn up the fighter instinct *and* embrace their gentler side. These men possess grit, courage, long-suffering, and strength. They are also humble, kind, and generous. They are loving fathers and vulnerable husbands, considerate but deliberate leaders. Be that kind of man, the unlikely combination of warrior and poet.

PRACTICUM

Get real with yourself. Have you cultivated or repressed the Warrior Within?

When did you last feel that call to fight?

Envision what your life would look like if you came fully alive, if you embraced your own warrior spirit completely, instead of shrinking back when the world tries to coax it out of you.

How would your life change if you summoned the courage to be who you know you should be?

2

The Most Dangerous Man in the Room

If you know the enemy and know yourself, you need not fear the result of a hundred battles. If you know yourself but not the enemy, for every victory gained you will also suffer a defeat. If you know neither the enemy nor yourself, you will succumb in every battle.

—SUN TZU

Tony Lopez was our high school Spanish teacher and the coach of the girls' soccer team. When you saw this man, there was nothing particularly impressive about him. He was neither scary-looking nor intimidating. A man in his forties with a bit of a gut, he wore thick-rimmed glasses and had a quiet and friendly disposition. He did not appear to be dangerous to me—not at all.

When I first met Mr. Lopez, I was a good wrestler and knew it. As a puffed-up senior, I was all confidence and ego. My whole identity was wrapped up in my ability to wrestle another guy to the ground and overcome him. Coupling my physical talent with an abundance of teenage testosterone, I had fallen into a habit of sizing up every dude I came in contact with. It's not a thing I'm proud of.

When I saw Mr. Lopez, I saw a man who didn't threaten me one bit. I did not believe he could last more than a few seconds in a fight with me. No way. Having already played out the whole scene in my head, this guy, like many others, would have no idea what hit him. This was my habit, in case that sounds crazy. I was always sizing up other people, looking for a fight and playing out every detail of it to be one step ahead of whoever my combatant might be.

Anyway, one day, Mr. Lopez came to our wrestling practice, and I learned that he taught a martial art called combat sambo. He was looking for a workout that day and decided to join the wrestling team. My coach paired the slightly portly Spanish teacher with me for some drills and I was, to put it mildly, not thrilled. I was certainly going to yawn through my decimation of this man.

We started running through the drills Coach called out and as we started, Mr. Lopez politely started chatting with me. In the first minute, I discovered how much he could *move*—and quickly. I began adding a little resistance, pushing back, as he went about the practiced moves. When that didn't seem to slow the man down, I added more resistance, fighting back against Mr. Lopez a little harder. Then, I added a *lot* more resistance, and it still didn't seem to matter. Without stopping his chatting,

Mr. Lopez effortlessly glided past my defenses without any difficulty. It was mind-blowing.

I didn't understand what was happening. I was a champion. I was the school's best wrestler. I had annihilated guys that outweighed me by over a hundred pounds. And here I was, getting bested by a girls' soccer coach. It wasn't long until Coach moved us into free wrestling, and I tore at Tony like a savage, bringing out my A game. It didn't matter. Mr. Lopez destroyed me. More humiliating still, he kept chatting with me as we battled. He didn't even know this was an epic war in which I intended to give no quarter. He didn't know what was at stake. He was playing with me, having fun, barely breaking a sweat. To this day, I still have not recovered from that fight. He absolutely destroyed me and wasn't even fazed, leaving me panting on the mat, soaking in the sweat of my own embarrassment and defeat.

Who, exactly, *was* this guy?

He was, I have come to learn, the most dangerous man in the room. The lesson I learned that day on the mat was about fighting, sure, but it also taught me something about life. I realized that underestimating people was a grievous mistake. My ego, which felt like a strength of mine at the time, was actually quite fragile. And I learned that knowledge could beat speed, strength, and youth. Most of all, I learned that anyone could be a warrior, regardless of how they looked. It's good to be in great physical shape; but inner strength, wisdom, and training were far more important than any outward display of physicality. Mr. Lopez taught me that, and I hope to never forget it.

You may be able to run twenty miles and bench press a Ford Focus, but you won't get far without having the right character and the right attitude. Your habits and ambitions matter. Your values matter. What you are willing to live and die for is important, too. But the most important aspect of being a warrior is learning to become a truly dangerous man. And that may not mean what you think it does.

LET THEM UNDERESTIMATE YOU

When you think of the "most dangerous" men in a room, the obvious choices are the big guys tatted up wearing MultiCam with a Glock T-shirt and gun stickers all over their cars. When I see that sort of man, I typically think "good guy." We might even chat about what he's carrying, or he may even be a fellow member of the Warrior Poet Society.

But when I see a dude like that, I also see crosshairs all over him. For a bad guy, those are the easiest men to spot and take out immediately. With a guy like that, if you ever had to go toe to toe with him, you'd at least give him the respect of putting your best foot forward. In that kind of scenario, you'd want to attack hard and fast, bringing your absolute A game—because you know what he's capable of.

But not with men like Tony Lopez. Never would I have pegged *that* kind of man as someone to fear, and because of this, I wasn't ready. Part of the power of a man like that is because you have seen him out in public, and he's not scary. Remember, Tony was chatting it up with me: a fun-loving, Spanish-speaking, jovial man. Or so it seemed. I never would have dreamed what he was capable of, and that's what made him dangerous. It would be like going up to some bushes and seeing a little tail sticking out, then giving it a tug only to discover a massive Bengal tiger hiding behind the leaves.

That was Tony Lopez—he was the tiger.

And I was his prey.

Judging from appearances, I wouldn't have given this man the respect of getting into a fighting stance and giving it my all. And because of that, he got me. I was caught completely off guard. Tony was the kind of man you didn't see coming, and those are the scariest men you'll encounter, because you don't know what they're capable of. A man who is unpredictable almost always has the upper hand. When people look across the room at you and can then say, "I bet he's bad news," you've just become a little less dangerous.

In *The Art of War*, Sun Tzu wrote, "Let your plans be dark and impenetrable as night, and when you move, fall like a thunderbolt." What he meant by this was: *Be underestimated. Never let them see you coming.* Most people don't realize that almost everybody is easy to kill. If I thought about how *I* would kill me, I really have no chance of defending myself. That sounds stupid, but welcome to the games I play in my head. If everybody is vulnerable, especially when you lose your element of surprise, then victory is not just about hitting your target—it's about ceasing to become a target at all.

I never want them to see me coming. That's why I dress in a relatively nondescript way, wearing collared shirts and blue jeans when I'm out in populated areas. You won't see any gun stickers on my cars or anything like that. I learned this from Tony: *Don't stand out. Don't brag. Don't look dangerous. Be humble or you will be humbled.*

That's where real danger comes from.

When I first entered the military, I heard an odd expression that became something of a mantra. It was a road map to success, and now I'm giving it to you: Be the gray man. This means don't stand out. Don't bring attention to yourself in any way, not for being terrible and not for being awesome. Overachievers will not like this advice. After all, your parents raised you to "do your best," so this may grate on you. But here's a lesson on survival your momma didn't teach you: There's a time to stand out and thrive and there's a time to camouflage and survive.

In business, you want to stand out and thrive. Well, usually. With the IRS, of course, you'd like to blend in and not stick out at all. In war, though, you want to blend in with your surroundings. Don't give a bad guy a shiny target to aim at. In military training, drill sergeants will immediately notice those who stand out—for good or bad—and chastise them. The cost of being noticed in high-stakes environments can be measured in sweat and blood.

In life, it is the arrogant man who stands out and calls massive amounts of attention to himself. He alone does not realize that the rest of the world is not as in love with him as he is. People may look at the arrogant person with some sense of awe, but they are also hoping that person falls. Here, the humility of the "gray man" goes a very long way. This principle is not just a tactical strategy but one to live by in all areas of life. Stand out in the right ways at the right times. And don't stand out in the wrong ways at the wrong times. It's that simple.

There was a leadership course I completed in the Army called the Primary Leadership Development Course, or PLDC. This is where you go to become a noncommissioned officer and attain the rank of sergeant. As I excelled in this course (due to the influence of the high-stakes environment of Ranger Battalion), I forgot to shift gears to gray man mode.

As a result, I stood out in all the good and bad ways one can. I was literally up for "honor graduate" and for expulsion from the course *at the same time*! I don't think that's ever been done before, but yours truly pulled it off. Wisdom is knowing when to stand out for good (e.g., integrity, business, athletics) and when to blend in (e.g., war, taxes). Suffice to say, my time in PLDC wasn't pretty and I barely survived my own by standing out. Since then, I've learned to be the gray man on a daily basis. And my life is better for it.

WHY WE NEED DANGEROUS MEN

The world is built—and ruined—by dangerous men. Men who take risks. Men who go against the grain. Men who are righteous lions and vicious serpents. We remember these men, for better or worse, for they are our very own villains and heroes.

We celebrate them as well as denigrate them, depending on the circumstance. But these are the men who make things happen, regardless.

As a society, we have applauded and reviled them, thanking men for their sacrifices and warning the next generation of their existence. We put their faces on our dollar bills and their names on our buildings but quickly forget their contributions. In one generation we build statues of them in thanks, and in a later generation we curse their names and rip down the monuments of them. The world is the way it is, right or wrong, due to the work of men who know their strengths.

World War II demanded a man who was ready to die on principle, despite insuperable odds. The world required a certain kind of soldier to stand in the way of tyrants and unblinkingly scream, "Die, Nazi scum!" This was not a soft man. He was not merely a "nice guy." Facing our potential extinction, we as a society cherished these men, celebrating them with parades and jobs and gratitude. But then, the war ended and that warrior was no longer needed.

Two decades later came the Vietnam War. This time, the people demanded a different kind of man. These were easy times, and the world wanted a softer man. "Make love, not war," was the cultural sentiment. After seeing the atrocities of the Holocaust and the shocking death toll of the atom bomb, we wanted distance from the horrors of war. We found solace in psychedelic drugs, bell-bottoms, peace signs, and pacifism. The times demanded a harmless man, and therefore the very warriors who went to fight in the name of freedom were rejected by their homeland.

Now, the soldier in Vietnam has my special sympathy because he not only had to have the strength of a soldier at war but also had to endure the hate of his nation while he defended it. The vitriol of the war protestors, though perhaps meant for political leaders, was borne on the backs of despairing soldiers.

I don't care to comment on whether we should or shouldn't have been in Vietnam in the first place, because my point is really only about the soldiers in the trenches and the civilians that waited back home. Many war veterans returned not to the applause their parents received when coming back from World War II but instead to crowds literally spitting in their faces. It is so unjust and so sad to break a man's heart. In fact, it did just that, breaking the hearts and spirits of our warriors.

The author G. Michael Hopf wrote, "Hard times create strong men. Strong men create good times. Good times create weak men. And, weak men create hard times." We see this cycle repeated throughout history for as long as there have been civilizations to speak of. You can observe it happening in the rise and decline of empires, all following the same tragic pattern.

In many ways, we are still living in those days of increasingly easy times, especially in America, which is producing softer men each day. This is not good. Mainstream culture continues to shift toward relativism and acceptance of atrocities that would have embarrassed our forefathers. The moral absolutes of yesterday are chalked up to a dated naivety. God is rejected. Patriotism is scorned. The family structure is being dissolved. Even the lines of gender, which have been intrinsically understood since the dawn of humanity, have been thrown into question. Everything we have known and held dear seems to be slipping between our fingers.

This is not an "out there" kind of problem. It is here and now, and things are only getting worse. As we sit in the lap of luxury during the most affluent age that has ever existed, we do so with front-row seats to our own forthcoming apocalypse. That may sound grim, but history teaches that comfort never remains a default. Liberty invites violence from outsiders who want to steal what they did not earn. Affluence attracts envy, and those with the most should not be surprised when someone comes knocking.

The freedom we have was fought for and must be protected. This is the way it has always been. We have a choice regarding what kind of world we want to create for our children, and we must choose it now, before it's too late. Unless we do something, we are headed toward the same fate as the men who lived to see empires crumble.

To build a better world, we need what we've always needed: Dangerous men. Men who are capable of violence. Men who can protect the weak and offer strength to the vulnerable. Men who know how to keep a society safe and free. Because the only way to defeat a bad man is with a good one who's even more dangerous. For the sake of your loved ones and the fate of the free world, you've got to become the most dangerous man in the room.

TRAITS OF DANGEROUS MEN

How do you tell a hero from a distance? Good question. They don't always look the way you'd imagine them. A hero is someone who is virtuous and prevails against evil. Heroes are both dangerous and good. I've noticed a few qualities in the most dangerous dudes I know, a lot of who are in the "good guy" camp, but you can be dangerous without being good. We want both traits. Generally, these men have a certain set of qualities and characteristics. Once you know what to look for, you'll be able to spot a dangerous man when you encounter one.

First off, *dangerous men are tougher than a two-dollar steak.* (I've always wanted to work that phrase into a piece of writing.) This is not just tough-as-nails physical strength we're talking about but a mental and emotional grit. They'd rather die than quit, which is asinine but true. They don't complain much, seemingly impervious to discomfort. They live disciplined lives and can endure all kinds of pain without showing weakness. Of course, they still experience pain but have learned to bear it with a smile. These men have graveyard humor—they can laugh in the face of death—which itself is evidence of mental toughness. They can laugh at loss, not taking themselves too seriously or feeling too intimidated by risk.

Second, *dangerous men can manage fear better than most.* In the world of tactical training classes, where I work, the best instructors harp on a "fighter mindset," because they realize a secret others don't: it doesn't matter how strong you are if fear shuts you down. Managing fear is a monster; in fact, it's the big monster in every fight. The enemy is really just a small guy hiding behind our monstrous fears and insecurities. That's the inner coward we will talk about later—he'll get you when you're least expecting it if you don't watch him carefully.

Of course, everyone *thinks* they will rise to the occasion. We can all imagine ourselves winning and acting heroically, but it's uncommon for a person to do this without intentional training and preparation. When real fear shows up, most tend to shut down. It's the hero who can manage their own breathing, focus their mind on solving the next problem, and take another small step.

We all want to do this, but it's far from innate. Knowing if someone will do well in the face of fear can be known only by watching them. This is where experience leaves the pack behind and stands tall. I'm far less impressed these days by a person's physique and talent compared to a man I know will work well amid fear and chaos. That's the real person I want on my team; that's the man I would follow.

Third, *dangerous men are clever.* Dangerous men can think like a bad guy—sometimes, they *are* the bad guy. As creative problem solvers, even under enormous stress, they understand the fight is a game and the spoils don't always go to the strongest—they go to the smartest. Dangerous men understand not only the value of being in the right place at the right time, but also of doing the right thing at the right time. They can see what's coming before it happens. The most dangerous men, whether they're psychopaths, undercover agents, or genuinely good guys, aren't stupid.

Finally, the last trait worth mentioning is that *dangerous men know how to break you in a hundred different ways.* Whether that's striking you with their fists or using weapons, dangerous men are constantly war-gaming a thousand different ways to destroy their enemies. The minutiae of how to twist a human into a pretzel is a fun mental game to this person. Shaving a millisecond off a pistol draw is thrilling. These men are trying to become more skilled, because the more dangerous they can be, the greater advantage they have. The dangerous person not only has the mind that can destroy you but the skills to bring you to a swift end at any time.

CHOOSING TO BE DANGEROUS

Aggression in our culture is largely discouraged. As a man, you are told to be funny, compliant, and sensitive—but never dangerous. These days, the pendulum of masculine extremes is no longer swinging back and forth. It has swung hard to the left and been stuck in place for some time now.

You are told to soften your tone and approach, to do more yoga and get in touch with your body while at the same time being discouraged from being too confrontational, too bold, and too dangerous. When you take on the "nice guy" persona, however, you are no longer a leader, no longer dangerous. And who will follow such a man?

We have lost what it means to be masculine in the modern world, which will only serve to erode the stability of society, making us vulnerable to both physical and ideological attacks. Little boys run away from pain when their fathers haven't taught them how to deal with it, and we have an entire generation doing just that. When a man fears discomfort, danger is not far off.

What we need now is more boldness, not less. We need you to befriend what makes you dangerous. It's time to reject the low bar of being a "nice guy" and embrace a deeper, truer identity. We need dangerous men in the world, plain and simple. As psychologist and bestselling author Jordan Peterson writes, "A harmless man is not a good man. A good man is a very, very dangerous man who has that under voluntary control."

What do we do when the world asks us to be soft, but we recognize an inner call to be more than cuddly teddy bears? These days, it's not a bad idea to do the opposite of whatever culture says. When the latest woke celebrity tells you to do something, just do the opposite. Nowadays, when everything seems so upside down, the safest option is to choose your strength, own your dangerousness, and befriend your ferocity.

My friend Ryan Michler, founder of the Order of Man, recently summarized the current state of manhood: "We have to *choose* to be men in this day and age," he told me. "We don't have threats. We don't have existential crises that we're worried about. We don't have things that are gonna potentially derail us. The most catastrophic thing we might run into is potentially getting a little fender-bender or somebody getting upset or losing a client.

"We just don't know how to handle ourselves and take care of the things that need to be taken care of," he continued. "I've seen grown men crumble at the slightest sign of adversity because they don't place themselves under any sort of voluntary hardship. The more you can place yourself in that voluntary hardship, the more you inoculate yourself against the crises that will eventually inevitably come up."

For thousands of years, Michler explained, we've been "battling woolly mammoths and saber-toothed tigers." But now, our biggest challenge is work. "Come on," he sneered, "this is horse crap." It's good to have first-world problems as opposed to basic threats to our survival. "This is what we've worked toward. We're at the pinnacle of human achievement with medical advancements and technology and relative safety and more people out of poverty than ever."

We have access to life-saving medical technology and all kinds of other comforts that would have been an embarrassment of riches to our forefathers. But with all this advancement, we've made things too easy on ourselves, which has made most modern men soft. "We don't know how to handle order," Michler concluded. And he's right.

Most men are uneasy with the seeming ease of everyday life. They're bored. So they retreat into video games and sexual addictions and one too many glasses of whiskey at the end of the day—anything to numb the pain of not living up to their potential.

It's normal to seek adventure wherever men can find it, even if in fiction. Every man has a favorite movie, and most men tend to pick an action movie that almost always includes a strong warrior who aspires to a noble ideal. Without fail, this hero has a love interest, some sort of damsel worthy of his sacrifice, as well as a cause worth his life. Whether it be *Braveheart*, *Gladiator*, or *Star Wars*, these stories speak to us. They remind us of something sacred and profound we can still sense within.

Consider for a moment the strength of the hero from your favorite movie. I'd wager that it goes beyond mere physicality, as he risks life and limb to free others from tyranny and oppression. He could not do this if he were not dangerous, if he did not cultivate his inner and outer strength. This is what makes him heroic. He's not entirely safe, but he's also not a chaotic mess. He's disciplined.

As men, we must deepen our capacity for hardship, becoming more dangerous so that the dangers of life do not scare us away. We have to get out of our comfort zones, which means occasionally leaving our screens behind, doing stuff that scares us, and sometimes putting ourselves into harm's way. This is how we get braver and tougher—by doing hard things.

Choosing to be dangerous means admitting what you are capable of: understanding how bad you can be, the power you possess as a man. Every man is capable of violence, especially the one who doesn't know it. A man like that will inevitably hurt and abuse women. He will neglect young ones and poorly lead others. To be a good man, you can't deny the danger in you; you have to take control of it. A weak man cannot do this, because it takes strength to be good. And only a man who understands his own violence and how to temper it is truly safe.

So, to be safe, you've got to be dangerous. To be strong, you've got to understand your own weakness. This is the way of the Warrior Poet, a path riddled with contradictions, calling you to an ideal that you will spend the rest of your life pursuing.

HEROES, WIMPS, AND VILLAINS

All men are dangerous in different ways. There are, however, three distinct forms of a dangerous man, and we would be wise to recognize who we are up against so that we know what to do.

The first kind of dangerous man is a nefarious man, what we might call a villain. This is a true "bad guy" in every sense of the word. A person like this is someone who aims to injure other people. He can inflict pain on others and often does so through an ambush, something that doesn't require him to be particularly strong or skilled, much less brave. Nearly anyone can be dangerous if they're hostile. The villain deliberately wants to cause pain and suffering. I don't want to give them more space in this book than they deserve, because these men suck. I only hope they can meet the third type of dangerous man—which we'll discuss shortly.

The second type is the wimp. This man is not dangerous because he's strong but quite the opposite. In his greed and cowardice, the wimp will betray another and not even know it. Because of his weak disposition, he will hurt others accidentally, clumsily wrecking everything around him without much aware-ness of the consequences at all.

As this man moves through life idiotically, without any dis-cipline whatsoever, he will cause a lot of damage. His behavior is often excused because he seems to mean well. People don't want to charge wimps with real wrongdoing because wimps present themselves as victims. They may seem like sweeties until they have an opportunity to betray, cheat, lie, or steal. And they will always take the easy wrong instead of the hard right. When Peterson says there is no one more dangerous than a weak man, this is the worm he's talking about.

Sadly, I don't hear many people calling these men out, be-cause they're safeguarded by society. I think people consider it bullying to call out a weak and bad man; but before you jump on that bandwagon, remember that all of the world's pedophiles hang out in this category. A weak man is worse than a nefarious one, because he destroys from within as a presumed ally. He cannot repent of the sins he refuses to acknowledge, and the longer we allow such neglect, the longer we deprive our world of men who could be good if they only knew how bad they were.

The third type of dangerous man is the hero. This is the ideal of dangerousness to which we all aspire. This man is not only capable of lovingly protecting others, he considers it his sacred duty to do so. These men are sacred guardians of their homes and nations; they utilize their strength and courage and attack injustice wherever they see it. They are brave and selfless, or at least they aspire to be. It's only under the shadow of men like this that freedom can possibly survive.

To be heroic is to be more than strong. Just because someone can hit hard or lift a ton of weight or shoot well doesn't mean much. These abilities won't tell you anything about a man's goodness. They don't reveal his character, which is what matters most. A real hero is somewhat separated from society; he and his fellows hold themselves and one another to a code. They live by and for a higher purpose, which means normal people are safe around them. Children don't need to fear such men, and by following the hero's example they'll actually grow up to be better adults, because this influence helps kids become stronger; it emboldens them, inspiring them to become heroes in their own right.

DON'T BE RECKLESS

Remember *Top Gun*? In the original film from the eighties, a hotshot Navy pilot named Pete Mitchell (played by Tom Cruise) goes by the call sign Maverick and lives up to his moniker. Early in the movie, he's in the locker room next to the top-of-the-class pilot Iceman (played by Val Kilmer), and the two are in a moment of heated debate.

The men come chest to chest, tensions high, everyone around them watching. In the iconic scene, Iceman says in a clear act of confrontation to the young hotshot, "You're everyone's problem. That's because every time you go up in the air, you're unsafe. I don't like you because you're dangerous." Iceman meant it as an insult, but Maverick steps up even closer, nose-to-nose, and says, "That's right, Ice . . . *man*. I am dangerous." The scene is broken up by a commanding officer, and the two men disperse along with the rest of the onlookers. But there is a palpable feeling following that moment in the movie that cannot be overlooked or forgotten.

Maverick recognized that *dangerous* was a good thing. As reckless as he was, he understood that you want a dangerous pilot in the sky, a fighter who's less safe than the enemy. Now, to be fair, Iceman had a fantastic point. He was absolutely right in that you need to harness your wildness. But Maverick was right, too—you can't do away with what makes you dangerous and still defeat evil.

He was the right kind of dangerous, the kind that made the other pilots a little uncomfortable but got the job done. There is a fine line between being dangerous and reckless, and Maverick walked it well. In the end, he was the man for the hour. When things got bad, he was the hero we needed in such times. The cowboy. The rogue. The outcast. These are the men who keep the civilized world in balance by meeting their violent counterparts.

The film starts with Maverick being too reckless, though, not yet learning how to manage his own power. After the loss of his best friend and partner, he quits the military and opts for a safer life, thinking this will keep him from more loss. But that never works. When we don't maintain our own dangerous edge, the danger comes knocking. In those times, we need a real maverick. The hero must come out of self-imposed exile and remember what he is capable of.

In the final scene, Iceman calls to Maverick, who has just saved the day: "You! You are still dangerous. But you can be my wingman anytime." He's saying, *Now I trust you*. This is the arc of all heroes and the arc of our lives. There is a moment when Maverick doesn't trust his power and chooses to be less dangerous. Such weakness almost costs him and everyone their lives.

We don't need men who are safe; we need men who know how powerful they are. We will never be rid of terrorists, rapists, murderers, home invaders, muggers, gang members, or drug cartels. Almost every generation has seen a war or conflict in its time—and this is true even in the most affluent places on Earth.

My great-grandparents saw World War I, and my grandparents saw World War II. My father's generation saw Vietnam, and I have seen the Global War on Terrorism. What will my kids see? Strangely, we never seem to think the next bloody conflict will come until it drops right into our laps. In fear, we'd rather deny for the present and future, what history has warned is certain.

When facing a deadly enemy, we praise the men who protect us, but when there are no enemies at the gates, these same warriors become our greatest threats. We want men to be sensitive sweetie pies in times of peace but then call on these same men when danger arrives. We want guns to protect us when we feel vulnerable but ban them when we feel safe. The warrior can survive war, but how can he ever survive peace? The society saved by the hero almost always rejects the one who saved it.

People love to feel safe, and the presence of dangerous men reminds us that we are not as safe as we want to believe. A comfortable nation tries to tame its warriors, remolding them in the image of whatever is in vogue. If they don't comply, we reject them, cast them out, *cancel* them. We marginalize our brutes because they scare us. Then, it is only a matter of time before we are vulnerable and need dangerous men once more.

GOOD, BUT NOT SOFT

There are times, of course, when we need men to be something other than dangerous, when gentleness and kindness are completely called for. These are traits that are just as good as being able to clear a room or break a man's jaw. I've learned some of them the hard way. I know now from the book of Proverbs that "a gentle answer turns away wrath" and that it's my wife's gentle love that sets my will like flint to protect and provide for her, to romantically pursue her. I am keenly aware of the power of gentleness, and there is absolutely a time and place for it.

My own personal hero, Jesus of Nazareth, came into the world in gentleness, arriving as an innocent baby in a world full of violence. He was betrayed and murdered by evil men—and even allowed it to happen. It was His care for the sick and poor and His message of love that ignited the movement that became Christianity. An act of gentleness in the face of heinous violence

resulted in the world's largest religion. Billions of future followers would be wooed by this man's message of love and forgiveness. It was this gentle kindness that overthrew many stubborn
men, including myself.

Another example is Martin Luther King Jr., who was also
assassinated for his beliefs and message. King was not a warrior
in the traditional sense. Powerful in his words, sure, but he was
gentle in his approach, willingly letting bad men unlawfully
drag him away more than once to jail. His nonviolent approach
is what inspired many people to join the fight for racial equality
in America. Even though he was murdered for his message, his
peaceful protest eventually brought down the hatred and violence of outrageous discrimination.

I could go on and on, but the point is that love motivates a
warrior. Violence untethered to love is cold and meaningless.
Ecclesiastes tells us there is "a time to kill, and a time to heal . . .
a time for war, and a time for peace." We need dangerous men
who are compelled and controlled by goodness and self-sacrifice.
Anything less is not worth living for and certainly not worth
dying for.

Each warrior needs to know his calling from moment to moment, when he ought to be delicate and when he needs to come
down hard and fast on the enemy. I would not sit gently by and
watch a home invader rape and murder my family. Real love
protects, and there's a huge difference between turning the
other cheek to one who has insulted me and killing terrorists
who are trying to kill innocent people. My faith tells me that the

same God who died on a cross also led the charge at Jericho and issued armies to retake the Promised Land. This same Savior, according to the Bible, will come back not as a lamb but as a lion.

All of which is to say, you need to be both gentle *and* dangerous to be truly good.

THE STUFF KINGS ARE MADE OF

True masculinity has been all but lost in our modern world, but it still flows deep in our veins. We just need to wake up to what we could be, understanding what it means to be disciplined and strong, to be truly dangerous. As protectors, we want to carefully study the villain and the wimp so that we can see them for what they are. We also want to be more dangerous than the bad guys so we can keep them from causing harm. But through all this, we ultimately want to be the gray man, the most dangerous man in the room, the man who doesn't stand out until he absolutely has to.

We Warrior Poets want our gentleness to be aligned with our violence and vice versa, knowing when it's time to strike and when it's time to dance. And above all, we strive to be good. That's what Tony Lopez was to me: a man who could tear me apart piece by piece and do so with humility. He modeled a gentle and calmer strength I had not seen up close and personal before.

In C. S. Lewis's classic *The Lion, the Witch and the Wardrobe*, there's a memorable scene where the children are about to meet

Aslan, the anthropomorphized lion and hero of the story. It goes like this:

> "Aslan is a lion—the Lion, the great Lion."
>
> "Ooh!" said Susan. "I'd thought he was a man. Is he—quite safe? I shall feel rather nervous about meeting a lion." . . .
>
> "Safe?" said Mr. Beaver . . . "Who said anything about safe? 'Course he isn't safe. But he's good. He's the King, I tell you."

This is our standard: the messianic figure of Aslan, the Great Lion. He is not safe, but he is good. And that's what we need to press into. In the story, we see Aslan as gentle and loving but also as wild and savage. These coexistent traits set my soul on fire. I cannot stand how much I love this lion who inspires me to be the man I'm supposed to be. This is what it means to be a warrior and a poet and—at the risk of sounding a little dramatic—a king.

PRACTICUM

Do something physical a few days a week.

Work out.

Take jiu-jitsu or kickboxing classes.

Shoot guns and seek out professional training in learning to fight.

Play a sport (preferably contact, but at least competitive).

Do something dangerous. Start small, valuing consistency over quality.

As your habit forms, you can get into more intense activities and scale up the frequency.

Stop living vicariously through the exploits of athletes, actors, and video game avatars.

Become what you admire.

Train the Warrior Within, so that when the time of battle comes, he is ready.

3

Battle the Inner Coward

Cowards die many times before their deaths; / The valiant taste of death but once.

—WILLIAM SHAKESPEARE

When I was around eleven years old, I was on a group trip to Six Flags amusement park. This place was a thrill-seeker's dream, filled with crazy rollercoasters with all the loops and spins and speed you could ask for. At this park, there was a certain ride called the Great American Scream Machine. No upside-down, crazy corkscrew turns or anything like that; it was just a fast roller coaster. And it scared me.

As I stood in line with my friends, getting closer to the front, I began to feel nervous. When I took a seat on the ride and the latch descended on my lap, locking me into this commitment, I panicked. I started freaking out and asked the operator to lift the bar so that I could get off the ride. This caused the bar to have to be lifted for everyone. Little girls stayed on the ride, and I chickened out. To this day, I'm still shamed by my own cowardice.

The worst enemy we face in life is always ourselves. *You* are the biggest obstacle between where you are now and the courageous life you are capable of living, the one calling to you. We all have an "inner coward," a voice that tells us when to play it safe and look out only for ourselves. This is the part of us that avoids conflict, that shies away from ruffling feathers, and sometimes hesitates to speak the truth.

As men, we are meant to bear burdens, and these obligations are anything but comfortable. Of course, we have a part of us that would prefer to bypass such difficulty. I carry a timid "lawyer" in my head, a character I've named Mr. Reasonable (no offense to lawyers, except those who deserve it). I hear him pop up on occasion and levy all kinds of excuses about why I don't need to do the right thing. Often, Mr. Reasonable keeps me safe and prevents me from being an absolute idiot. But if he got his way every time, he would have me neutered. It has taken me years to know when to listen to Mr. Reasonable and when to tell him to shut up and pound sand.

Every man has some "lawyerly" self that tries to weasel out of any potential conflict or challenge. We all have what the apostle Paul called "the flesh," which is our own fearful and weak nature. This enemy seeks safety, coddling, and a conflict-free life. He skirts around responsibility, because responsibility will at some point cause pain.

Many have fallen prey to the gospel of political correctness that tells us to be nice, all while silencing our courage. Entire empires have collapsed as a result of a leader listening to his inner coward, asking what others might do instead of demanding what is required. We have seen the enemy, my friends, and he is us. To become good men, we must face our own inner coward, learn to do hard things we would rather avoid, and cultivate our strength.

THE MANY FACES OF COWARDICE

There is nothing wrong with being afraid, of course. What you do with it is what separates the cowards from the heroes. Naturally, the temptation to give into what we fear can take many shapes and sizes. To become a Warrior Poet means committing to honing your emotional, mental, spiritual, and physical strength. Bravery starts in the heart then ripples through our whole being. Before we can go to battle on behalf of others, then, we must face our own fears. This is always, initially, an internal struggle.

I've known mixed martial artists who had zero fear of fighting dangerous men but were terrified to the point of being mute when it came to talking to girls. In their defense, women are scary; but fear finds our weak points and presses hard. We have to learn to endure the pressure.

I knew a retired Special Forces soldier who was scared to death of legal contracts. This mysterious area of the civilian business world was so upsetting to him that I watched him walk away from a good opportunity simply because he was terrified of signing a dotted line. When I asked my friend about this, he said that he could run toward gunfire without a second thought, but contracts freaked him out.

Fear can steal our hearts and minds, freezing us into inaction. It can send us running when we should stand our ground. Temporarily vanquishing one insecurity in one area of your life doesn't mean this elusive enemy is held at bay for long.

A man's inner coward does not go away. He is not defeated forever; once you face him, you start to see his wiliness. If you are successful, he will hide in the shadows until the next moment. Be careful of this coward, because he is always lurking right around another corner, looking for a way in. It's your job to practice courage, and this takes time and discipline.

One way to stay on top of such an enemy is to face what you are afraid of. Find regular ways to make your mind, body, and soul stronger. Human beings don't naturally get wiser or braver just because; it's only through confronting difficulty and danger that we learn to adapt to the harshness of the world around us. We need to regularly test our strength and toughen our minds and bodies. If we are not strong, both inside and out, we will give fear the foothold it needs to take root and then grow and grow. Don't give it an inch.

Strangely enough, sometimes cowardice finds us not when we are at our lowest, but when we are at our highest. Sure, we get scared when we are backed into a corner and defeated, but the book of Proverbs also cautions that "a man is tested by his praise." When we are in our greatest place of authority or prestige, we can be terrified of losing what we have. This can lead to the cowardly compromise of values, or it can lead to puffing ourselves up with pride (which leads to a fall). Whether we are high or low, cowardice will come; it just wears different clothes, or sometimes none at all.

This reminds me of a great king of Israel and a gifted poet who lived three thousand years ago. Though he certainly made grievous and horrible mistakes in life, this king sought forgiveness for the ways in which he gave in to his own fears and temptations. If you don't know the story, the Israelite King David allows a man to be killed so that he can take his wife, whom he has already slept with and impregnated. It's not good, not at all. Humbled by his shortcomings, David repents of his sins and does everything he can to make right what cannot be made right.

Though David's conduct was inexcusable and terrible, there is something to be said for the fact that he repented and lived to be a much better man and king than before. The point is that he was a great man who fell hard and played the coward, but he repented and rose again. If there was hope for David, then there is hope for you and me.

A good man is honest about his shortcomings; he grieves the damage he has caused others, feeling the consequences of his own stupidity. In David's case, he was heartbroken over his own cowardice. He knew he had screwed up and lost the battle for his own integrity. He knew he would have to fight for the rest of his life to stay true to the goodness he sought. And he did. When a man gives in to one of either extremes—the warrior or the poet—he is imbalanced and prone to cowardice. An effete poet will run from the threat of violence just as quickly as an insensitive jerk will shy away from emotional conflict.

Today, we live in a society that has lost its sense of what it means to be masculine. King David would write heart-wrenching poems and hold deep and vulnerable friendships with other men, yet still turn on a dime to stack bloody Philistine bodies when it was time for war. He had a deep devotion to God, which he would credit as the source for his strength, giving him the courage needed to fight against the evils of his day.

Though I am not worthy to be mentioned close to such a man, I also believe in a source of strength greater than myself, which allows me to embrace both my inner lover and outer fighter. My faith in God provides a context for my own tendency toward self-centeredness and cowardice; it gives me a map to navigate these conflicting paths, as well as a model for what a true man is.

I know how far short I fall from the ideal, and this keeps my feet on the ground and my heart focused on improving myself each and every day. I have not arrived and never will. But I can continue to strive for something better than what I am today.

BECOMING BRAVE

These days, we're not flooded by many examples of the brave masculinity I've been speaking of. For me, it is far easier to find good men in the past—in old stories and literature as well as in our very own history books—than to seek them in the present.

To be sure, there are Warrior Poets among us; but they are few and far between (for now). However, when we dive into the world of our ancestors, we see these ideals repeated over and over again.

The great British philosopher and Christian apologist G. K. Chesterton was once asked, "What's wrong with the world?" and his response was, "I am." He understood that at the core of everything is a pull toward the self. I believe the root of all evil is pride. C. S. Lewis calls pride the very center of Christian immorality. It is easy to be self-centered, and it is quite difficult to care more for others. It is easy to play the coward in seeking to validate our own egos and desires, and it is unbearably hard to humbly love and serve others.

I know what cowardice is because I have played the coward many times in my life. What makes the world a bad place is the compounding effect of men and women looking out primarily for themselves and passing the buck on to someone else. What we see in the examples of other heroes is a willingness to die. To lay down their lives for the sake of others. This is the ultimate sacrifice: to let go of your hardwired instinct to take care of just you and offer your life to something greater. This is true bravery.

Ironically, our desire to focus on ourselves is self-defeating. Selfishness separates us from the source of life itself and forces us to abandon who we are for the sake of something safe. When we make small compromises in our integrity over time, we slowly begin to abandon the part of ourselves required for the next battle. In any pursuit, a man will face the temptation to hide from what he fears instead of facing it head on, with humility, love, and courage.

Every good man must realize what a coward he is and how familiar such a position is. The antidote to cowardice is not courage; it's humility. Courage happens only after you've been honest with yourself about what you are and how far you've fallen short. You have to face how bad you are before you can begin to be good, you have to know what you are capable of and how close you are to being just another bad guy. And then, you can start to face the next enemy: your attachment to comfort.

Your body is a liar. At the first sign of discomfort, it yells, "Hey, I don't like this!" Then, when discomfort graduates to pain, the body screams, "I can't take anymore! I'm dying!" Our bodies are such drama queens. The body is like a spoiled and petulant child that cries out at the first moment its comfort is challenged. While babies get to evoke this right, need I contend that it is one of the most pathetic attributes in a man?

What I've found over the course of my life are a thousand different physical limitations—nearly all broken by grit. Whatever you think is a limit, do not be surprised that on the other side of that horrible moment is a little more ground you can cover. You are stronger than you realize, and you only need a test to prove it.

The human body can go about forty days without food. It can go three days without water. If you miss lunch, you won't die. I remember greedily searching trash during Ranger School for some food after they had rationed our calories to an extreme. We were starving, and trash food sounded better than nothing. We also found a chicken, killed it, and cooked it over a fire. Anyway, quit being a whining baby whenever you need a snack or are thirsty. You're fine.

The longest recorded length a person has gone without sleep is eleven days. If we have to sacrifice some shut-eye for family or work, we can do it. It will be uncomfortable, but no one will know because we know our bodies are liars, and we will ignore their whining.

Now, saying all this is far easier than doing it. I vividly remember going five days on a total of six hours of sleep in Ranger School. Yes, it's a far cry from eleven days, but I'm pretty sure I was burning more fuel than that guy! Doing hard things hurts. There's no way around it. Being cold, hungry, overworked, exhausted—it all just sucks, and there's really nothing to be done but swallow the complaints and take the pain. You can do this, because you are stronger than you know. You just have never met misery.

A FRIEND NAMED MISERY

As I mentioned, my background is in the Army, which culminated in joining Ranger Battalion, which is one of the most elite military operations on Earth. I have to be honest with you: basic training was a breeze. I saw the psychological games my drill sergeant played and thought the whole thing was amusing. Certainly, there were tough moments, but the whole thing seemed theatrical to me. I'd prepared my body for this, and for the most part, I was ready.

Ranger training was not the same. It was, for lack of a better word, horrifying. I was immediately picked out of a lineup of Rangers by an angry team leader who was waiting for us. He looked over our records, decided I was the one he wanted, and took me away from the other new recruits to join his team.

I remember my first day in Ranger Battalion vividly. It's funny looking back, though it wasn't funny at all going through it. I was led upstairs and down a hallway. I remember spotting a mural at the intersection of the hallway, and in it was a barbarian wielding an axe high above his head as he was about to kill an enemy. He was standing on a literal pile of dead people, and the mural's carnage stretched from floor to ceiling. *Kind of cool,* I thought, but also very ominous. I was likely to be a body in that pile before the day was done.

I was led into a room where my future squad was sitting around and thought, *Whoa, these are* real *Rangers.* All eyes were on me. I was being sized up. Would I prove myself to be one of them? They knew I had passed the tests to get to battalion, but I quickly realized they were going to do their own testing, and the testing was going to take a full year.

They wasted no time. The first agenda item was to pack me for war, so I was told to dump out everything I owned in the center of the floor for the squad to see. Then began the first game I ever played at Ranger Battalion. It was called Find It Before I Do.

In the game, my new team leader would read out an item by its crazy military nomenclature, and my instructions were to find it before he or the specialists did. The problem was I had no idea what LEPS Level IV was. I had absolutely no concept of what a VS-17 panel was. I didn't know anything. But the game was on.

My team leader read out the first item and I dove into the pile without hesitation. I rooted around for a moment then held up some random item. There was a moment of silence, and I thought that perhaps I had gotten incredibly lucky on my first try.

"Push-ups, LOVE-ellll," he called out. He never did pronounce my name correctly. I fell to my stomach to start pushing. This game continued for well over an hour until I had collapsed in a pool of my own sweat and a bag packed for war sat behind me. My team leader and the rest of the Rangers left the room, and I was alone with a couple fellow privates who had been in the squad for some time. They were a bit distant, but sympathetic, likely thinking back to when they first played the pain games.

For two weeks, I had no bed or even a locker. My stuff was shoved in a corner, and I slept on the couch. Every time I left the room, there was a good chance of running into some new, angry Ranger who was going to harass me for being alive and being too close to the air they were breathing.

A week later, I went on my first big training mission. It was an airfield seizure and our entire company was involved. It was about fifty degrees outside, maybe a tad colder, and it was raining. I was told to wear my normal BDU (battle dress uniform) top and no extra rain or cold-weather gear because we wouldn't be out there long enough to need it. I was given a rifle, a normal battlefield loadout, and every other heavy thing the squad wanted but didn't want to carry. Huge medical bags and awkward, heavy breaching tools hung off me like I was the loaded-down car from the Beverly Hillbillies.

Our squad members moved into position, and I followed their lead, trying to be quiet and keep up. We bounded across the airfield, cleared some buildings (I had zero idea what I was doing), then set up on the far side of the runway to wait for a plane to land, which would signal "mission complete."

I'm not sure whether my team leader did this deliberately or not, but when we got to the edge of the airfield, he pointed to a huge puddle and said, "Lay down there, LOVE-ell."

I had been pouring sweat up till this point, so the cold was of zero concern. I eased myself down into the puddle and immediately the cold water began its work on me. Within a couple minutes, I was no longer sweating. A few minutes after that, I was freezing. Fifty degrees isn't so bad when you are walking around town or going from your house to your car. But when you are wearing no warm clothes and are outside for hours, unable to move, and soaking wet, it can quickly feel like a death sentence.

My team leader was gone a long time as I shivered in that life-sucking puddle. When I finally did see him again, it was the first time I was ever happy to see him. He knelt beside me and said these horrible words, "The bird is running late. It's gonna be like . . . an hour." Then he was gone again. I was not new to games. The physical part of training was never as hard as the mental. It is the mind that quits first, under the suggestion of the body. But the body can endure horrible things if only the mind will lead it.

I smiled. *Yeah, right.* We'd all be dead of the cold by then. He was bluffing. I knew it. Nice try, Ranger.

After half an hour, I was in bad shape. My shivering seemed to have moved to full-body convulsions. Having now inched my way out of the puddle, I was still soaked to the bone, exercising in place to stay warm. To prevent my body from going into hypothermia, I held my body as straight as a board, putting all my weight on my toes and elbows. Then, I would squeeze my core and clench it until my muscles felt like they were on fire.

I had another trick up my sleeve. A blessed bag of Skittles was in my pocket. It was a treasure of sugared happiness to someone freezing to death alone in the dark. The problem was that my fingers had become so numb they no longer worked. Holding the bag in between my hands, I tried with all my might to tear it, but instead my fingers fell off the bag as if they were wet spaghetti noodles.

Crap, I thought. *I don't even get to enjoy my last meal.*

In a final, desperate attempt to taste the rainbow, I held the bag of Skittles between my two wrists and palms, bit the top of the bag, and tore at it. You've seen a dog bite into a chew toy then shake its head violently back and forth, right? That was my plan. If I was to die that night, my tongue would be red from Skittles rather than blue from hypothermia.

Victory! The bag peeled open, and I rationed out my sustenance until either the bird landed or death came for me.

I know you probably think I'm joking about the death thing, but I really was convinced that I was dying that night. After a long while, my body stopped shivering. I felt numb, but the pain of the cold was gone. I was accepting it. It wasn't so bad. That's when I knew hypothermia was setting in, and I needed to fight to keep my body heat up. I had been praying for God to save me, but somewhere in the fight against the cold, I resigned myself to the inevitable and my prayers shifted to, "Here I come, Jesus, thank You for the life You gave me."

When it was finally time to move out, nearly an hour after my team leader sank down to give me the bad news, we were pulled back off the line. I mustered all my strength, pushed myself up and saw the group of Rangers about twenty yards behind me, and I began to run toward them. I only started, though. My legs did not cooperate, and I dropped like a felled tree.

When I hit the ground, I was laughing. Up I went again to run, and again I wiped out. Somehow, I managed to shock life back into my legs and made it to a smaller huddle of Rangers to the side of a larger huddle. It was the other privates from my squad.

"Are you guys thinking what I'm thinking?" I asked.

"What's that?" one said.

"I would do anything for a snow cone."

We all laughed together in our misery. They were freezing to death, too, and immediately loved the joke. That night, I was welcomed into the squad by the veteran privates. We were in this together and we were all going to make it—together. We had made misery our friend, which in itself is an act of courage and the only way to fight off the inner coward for another day.

STAVING OFF SOFTNESS

A few years ago, my son scraped his knee and started crying. There was blood trickling down, and as he cried, I tried to comfort him: "It's not bad, buddy! I know it hurts!" Nothing helped. So I had a crazy thought. I pulled out my knife and proceeded to cut a line across my forearm. My boy immediately stopped crying and looked at me in astonishment. As blood dripped down my arm, I looked my son in the eyes and said, "This hurts me the same as yours hurts you. But I'm choosing to take the pain. I'm choosing to be tough. And I'm asking you to do the same."

At that moment, he officially finished crying. I believe he learned something my words alone couldn't teach. After that day, he was tougher, braver. I could see it in his eyes. He saw something that called him to a stronger version of himself. When he gets injured now, he wants me to notice how tough he is being, and I am all too excited to let him know how awesome he is doing. We all need examples of others who have endured hard things, showing us what's possible. Of course, there's nothing wrong with crying or displaying emotion when it comes to matters of the heart. Tears of joy and love are fair game, but if we break a bone we need to man up and tough it out in silent suffering.

We live in easy times, times that protect us from the harshness of the world. I am saddened to see many men giving in to the pressures of their culture and circumstances. The ease of a good life can soften a man to the point of making him vulnerable to all kinds of attacks and exploitation. The only way we keep such forces at bay is by continually leaning into adversity. To discipline our minds, souls, and bodies on a daily basis.

In movies and popular culture, we see stories with soft-eyed, super-sensitive guys piling up among the millions of other chick flicks that crowd our screens nowadays. This is doing a massive disservice to young men who are longing for an example to look up to. When we see an androgynous Harry Styles prancing around on stage in a dress to the praise of thousands at a time, we know we are in trouble.

Wherever we turn, we see what the poet Robert Bly called the "soft male" as the ultimate representation of modern masculinity. To combat this softness, we've got to endure situations that toughen up our physical bodies. We need strength to face the inner coward, and strength requires resistance. In other words, we have to do hard things. Face pain. Embrace the harsher demands of life, whether they be physical, spiritual, mental, or otherwise. We have to learn to bleed and smile, because we know others are watching.

Practically speaking, this means developing a set of daily disciplines to keep softness at bay. Lift heavy things that cause your body to strain. Go running farther than you think you can. Take cold showers and ignore that automatic response that says, "Get me out of here!" Don't eat food for a couple days. Have one hard conversation every day with someone you care about. Do what feels uncomfortable, hard, or even scary, and do it on a regular basis.

For my part, I'm working out, doing jiu-jitsu from time to time, participating in gunfighting training, and trying to steward the Warrior Poet movement with courage. When you have a large presence on YouTube and social media that helps run your business, it's scary doing stuff you know will tick off the Big Tech platforms that host your content. I have chosen to not play it safe but rather talk openly and boldly about issues I believe in deeply, like freedom from tyrants, my Christian faith, free speech, the pro-life movement, traditional masculinity, capitalism, and the Second Amendment.

Every time I talk about issues such as these, we see in our analytics that Big Tech downgrades the reach of our content. They have different values and do not want our values to spread. Not only have we felt the effects of demonetization, shadow bans, and censorship, but we also risk on a daily basis being removed from their platforms. We have other platforms we are engaged in that are more pro-freedom, but it's still a fear I have to push through. I used to be worried about roller coasters; now, it's a whole new set of challenges. The battle never ends—it only changes shape.

DIFFERENT KINDS OF STRENGTH

The call to be a whole man is an invitation, and one you do not have to accept. It is a rallying cry to a nearly-forgotten brotherhood—a call to arms, if you will, but also an invitation to surrender.

More and more, I see men waking up to this calling; they realize they can become more than they've been, and this doesn't mean only becoming physically stronger but also stepping into the best version of yourself you can be. We all have to face our own inner coward if we want to live a life worthy of our calling. This is a daily discipline, one that requires tremendous strength.

How do we become strong? By resistance, of course! Just like a muscle is strengthened by being worked and rebuilt, we've got to do the exact same thing in any area of life where we want to become stronger. It's a simple idea, but hard to execute. And of course, there are different ways to be strong.

Strength takes on many forms, depending on the context. For instance, you don't treat your spouse the same way you treat the soldiers downrange. Romance, patience, sensitivity, affection, compromise, and vulnerability are all critical to true strength. Relationships require a certain mental and emotional fortitude lacking in many men. Whether we're talking about cuddling your kids or taking your woman on a date, this is a kind of strength that takes practice. If you fail to adjust your definition of strong to fit the many different settings you experience in life, you will lose the very things that motivate you.

The shelf life of a soldier is often cut short by wrecked relationships collected over the course of careers filled with successful accomplishments. As a former Army Ranger, I've seen this over and over again. Relationships can be a pain in the neck and require a ton of attention and careful handling, but they are the reservoirs that keep you going in the long run.

Don't avoid difficulties, because they don't fit your "strong man" stereotype. We all have to challenge our areas of weakness if we want to become stronger. Consider these two missions in life: one is to be as tough as nails, as ferocious of a fighter as you can be, an absolute maniac; and the other is to be as kind and loving as possible, a giant so gentle that those you protect have no reason to fear you. We must always be battling our own short-comings so that we are getting stronger each day.

The Warrior Poet embraces all the ways he can be strong and understands that he is only as strong as his greatest flaw. Although your regimen will look different from mine, it may help to have a template. Throughout the week, I have a series of practices that help me face my own inner coward and cultivate the different kinds of strength every man has.

PHYSICAL STRENGTH

I work out three to five times per week and do various combat-related training in addition to these workouts. My workouts are fairly short (around twenty-five to forty-five minutes) and focus on a few minutes of warm-up cardio, body-weight exercises like push-ups, air squats, lunges, and pull-ups then maybe some moderate weight training. I'm more in the "ouch, my skeletal system is out of joint" season in life so my goals are more focused on practicality and rehab than crushing a new power-clean record. I will work out at all times of the day but usually in the early morning.

I have some friends who do the wake-up-at-four-and-work-out

thing, and I say bravo to them. But this is too great a sacrifice for me and not because I'm unable or unwilling to wake up early. A very early workout means that I'll need to go to bed earlier. But if I go to bed earlier, I will miss out on some of the most cherished time I have with my wife after the kids go to bed. To give more to my work productivity and workouts, I'd have to take time from my wife in this season of life. Later on, our schedules may shift, but for now, I'm healthier in the routine I have. Balance is the way.

I've also noticed that I'm most creative in the morning, so I protect those highly productive mental hours with the most important pieces of work that need to be tackled. This cuts my workouts a little short or I ditch them altogether if need be and get in my gym time later in the day as a way of shifting my headspace out of work mode. What I'm not attempting to do is convince you to adopt how I do things, but I do want you to be intentional about how you structure your day and about balancing between your competing priorities.

MENTAL STRENGTH

I read every single day. Sometimes, it's just a little bit. Sometimes, it's a lot. I'm always reading multiple books at a time and the books generally span different genres. Currently, I'm reading a book about the War of the Roses, as well as 2 Corinthians, Exodus, and Galatians in the Bible. My boys and I just finished a family reading of *The Last Battle*, which is the seventh and final book from C. S. Lewis's The Chronicles of Narnia series. About once a week, I'll pick up *A Patriot's History of the United States.* My intention with reading is to visit fiction books for creative inspiration and stress relief and to read nonfiction books for education.

I also listen to compelling speakers on YouTube and subscribe to a number of podcasts. I have deep conversations with friends about important issues on a regular basis, and work is a constant Rubik's Cube of problems to solve. All these keep my mind in shape, which does not happen by accident. This takes discipline and focus. Trust me when I say that scrolling your life away on the phone or binge-watching TV shows is working against you, not for you.

SPIRITUAL STRENGTH

As I've mentioned, reading the Bible is a daily discipline critical to my spiritual growth. Prayer is also a daily discipline of mine. The goal isn't to just pray before meals with the family but to "pray without ceasing," as the apostle Paul admonishes the Thessalonians in the New Testament. It's a difficult endeavor to be constantly praying in the back of your head as you go through the day, but that's the call—and it pays massive dividends.

Prayer is important to me, because I believe it not only moves God but it also moves me. Prayer helps to shape and replenish me in the most important of ways. I also gain spiritual strength each time I do the right thing, especially when it's difficult. At the same time, every instance I'm given to outbursts of anger, moments of self-centeredness, or harshness toward my family, my spiritual strength is sapped. Every action and thought moves us all toward greater spiritual strength or weakness, so . . . no pressure, right? HA! I didn't say any of this would be easy, gentlemen. I promise only that it will be worth it.

EMOTIONAL STRENGTH

This is something I don't have to hunt for in my life. I've got kids. I'm married. I'm running multiple businesses. I am saddled with so much weight and responsibility that my emotional strength is constantly being tested.

The more relationships (particularly the most meaningful ones) we have, the more emotional burdens we carry. Someone running from these relationships to lighten their own burdens can feel like they are improving their emotional health, but this is a fool's errand. If you offload the messy relationships and burdens that come with emotional commitments, you will later find you have eliminated most of your joy, loving connections, and the meaning that is found only in selfless care for another.

It is a challenge to connect with my family after a long day when I'm emotionally depleted. I often just want to space out, be alone, find silence, and have "me time." For what it's worth, I enjoy the occasional "veg out" time, but I would like to require less of it. Sometimes, a little TV time is just what I need, or sometimes it's a long walk, a workout, or a ride on one of my horses.

My desire to gain emotional strength is so that I can carry not only my own problems but the problems of others, as well. I want to have such a grip on my emotions that when I'm disrespected or maligned, cut off in traffic or experience any number of other perceived slights, I can keep my head. It is a weak man who is sent into a rage because someone didn't let them merge onto the highway, it is a child who rages when they don't get what they want.

It has been said that those who can anger you can control you, and I agree. I want to be in control of my emotions, attitudes, and moods, but I am not there yet. But I know where I'm weak and that my only real choice isn't in hiding from the burdens but in growing stronger so that I can bear them.

Wherever you are weakest, that is where you will be attacked. I've seen many physically strong men buckle under the weight of extreme physical pain, and I've seen other men with lesser physiques but far more mental toughness keep going. I've seen this with soldiers who I thought would do really well but who shocked me when they quit.

Muscles aside, there is a mental strength that allows us to endure pain. Emotionally, I've cracked under physical strain, and it makes me think of the many Christian martyrs over the millennia who were able to sing hymns while being flayed alive or sawed in two. There is a spiritual strength that allows one to go without food for long periods of time, endure torture, and face the imminence of certain death. I would like to be that strong, and I resolve to grow until I am.

Bearing up under any pain, physical or not, calls on the different types of strength we all possess. If any one of the chain links of physical, mental, emotional, and spiritual are too weak, the weakest link will snap when hardship comes—and with it, the man. He may have six-pack abs and can deadlift five hundred pounds, but if he cannot handle a little criticism, he's weak. If he crumbles into despair at the loss of a job, there is weakness in the chain. If he cannot handle the irritations every family brings, all can see his weakness. No shame here. I'm in these trenches myself. We have to continually test our strength so that we can stand on the day when it is needed most.

THE TESTING POINT

This is war, and war involves pain. You must be willing to endure pain of all kinds, especially that of your own cowardice. Begin by accepting the fact that there is a part of you that would rather run away and hide from the responsibilities of life than face whatever difficulties the day will present. Strength is required here, and this means you better embrace your own dangerousness (yes, it's actually a word).

Every man knows the voice of his own inner coward and the rationalizations that talk him out of potential hardship. Allow the discomfort of these experiences to sharpen you, to hone your natural desire for challenge and growth. Yes, we must be open-hearted, but too much softness makes warriors weak. A true protector needs to not only be strong but willing to suffer.

For too long, men have been backed into a corner and told to tone down their aggression. Little boys have been warned that their abundance of energy and excitement and thirst for adventure are flaws to be curbed. Sit still, our public schools tell them! And though we have times we sit still and study in our homeschool, we say let those boys run wild and free. They are learning something classrooms can't teach and that success in life requires.

Many of us have been hearing these voices for so long that we have started to internalize them, thinking it is the voice of our conscience or some divine force telling us to calm down. But if a soul desires to run wild and free, there is a time and a place to let it be.

This is the battle we are all born into: a world that hates what good men stand for and wants to eradicate every trace of masculinity. We are so used to these warnings that we don't even question them anymore, and as a result we have entire generations of men too scared to fight for what they really, truly believe in. Others are worse off and afraid to fight for anything at all.

"Courage," C. S. Lewis wrote, "is not simply one of the virtues but the form of every virtue at the testing point, which means at the point of highest reality." If that's true—and I believe it is—then that means before we can ever attempt to be good, we must first face our fear. Not all our fears all at once but the very part of us that is scared to fight.

Wage war against the wimp within. You cannot kill the inner coward; but you can keep him in check by doing hard things on a daily basis, including tackling your own selfishness, pride, and weakness. We face our cowardice not to overcome it but so that it won't overcome us. I have been in real gunfights in war and have seen the result turn out favorably. Looking back, I remember acting bravely and decisively, but I also remember the grip of paralyzing fear in other instances. I thought that if I could get to a point of bravery in battle, then I would always be able to perform in battle. It's a lie. Fear can grip anyone at any time, so our inner coward never dies and always must be challenged and faced.

To be aware of our proclivity to chicken out is an honest exercise; and from that place of humility, we can choose courage. Only then can we protect the vulnerable and comfort those in need. Courage, after all, is the testing point of all virtue. The world needs your strength, good man, but first it needs you to face the part of yourself that is too weak to stay on a roller coaster even little girls aren't afraid to ride.

PRACTICUM

This is going to be a simple assignment, but not an easy one. Do one thing that scares you. No, not whatever you're thinking of right now that's covering up the real thing you're afraid of. Do what you desperately don't want to do. Afraid of heights? Sign up for a ropes course, rock climbing, bungee jumping, or skydiving. This can be such a serious breakthrough for your life that it spills into all other areas. It is worth investing in and going for, trust me. Are you afraid to ask out the woman you've been eyeing for weeks? It doesn't matter if she accepts you. Your mission is to conquer fear, not get a date. Want to start a business? You don't have to quit your job; just take one step to start a side hustle that could one day become your livelihood. Run at what you are afraid of, and watch the fear shrink.

4

Face Death Before You Die

Do not go gentle into that good night. Rage, rage against the dying of the light.

—DYLAN THOMAS

The soldier knows a secret the average man doesn't: life tastes sweeter the closer to death you get. I've known many men who have come to grips with their own mortality long before it was their time to go and almost always have emerged better for it. These men now know what matters most; and when they live in accordance with this truth, their lives are fuller, richer, and deeper.

It's a cliché to talk about the captain of industry who, with millions of dollars to his name, goes to the grave unloved. On his deathbed, his net worth is irrelevant, his portfolio meaningless. What's important is to be reconciled with the grandkids he's been estranged from for decades, to mend the broken relationships he failed to repair earlier in life, and to seek forgiveness while he still can.

Close to death, this man knows that he'd trade everything for one more chance to make it right, to see the woman he once loved, to offer a heartfelt "Sorry" or "I wish I could have done more." If he only had more time, he'd gladly spend every second living life to the fullest. His accomplishments and accolades are now pointless; the size of his house and how many sports cars he has in the garage are like straw, ready to be burned away. He'd gladly spend his final days running through the streets shouting with joy like Ebenezer Scrooge. He'd be more generous, more loving, more kind.

The problem is it's too late.

Many men don't know the value of life until they face the end of it. The great gift of death is that it brings value to life, and the Warrior Poet knows this better than most. There is something transcendent about facing your own demise before it's too late. It's the only way to truly live, fully alive.

LIVE LIKE YOU'RE DYING

There's an old country song by Tim McGraw called "Live Like You Were Dying." The premise of the song is that a man gets a terminal cancer diagnosis and, now that he knows he's going to die, approaches life differently. He starts doing all the things on his bucket list—skydiving, mountain climbing, bull riding.

Trying to make the most of his remaining moments, he desires to live life with nothing held back. Before this realization, he doesn't know how short his life is; therefore, he doesn't know how to savor each morsel of his experience on Earth. Afterward, everything is different. Once death is close, he really starts to live.

When I first heard this song, I was in the military and smiled as I listened to it, realizing his bucket list was similar to my own. Because I have faced death many times, I've packed a lot of living into my life. Having gone to war five different times with Second Ranger Battalion, four times in Afghanistan and once in Iraq, each time I was required to write a "death letter" and put it inside my wall locker in the barracks.

We all had to do this. If you didn't come home, a buddy would mail your letter to your loved ones. So you had to make every word count. If you've never done something like this, it's no small thing. Writing the last things you will ever say to all the people you love most is something that will rock you to your core.

Before I sat down to write my first death letter, so many things mattered to me. Or so I thought. In writing the letter, I realized the stuff that mattered most made everything else seem trivial. As I wrote my last words to my family and friends, tears started flowing, muddying unlucky letters on the page as I realized those reading it would know I had loved them deeply.

Every man should do this at some point in his life, even if he isn't going off to war. Writing your own death letter is incredibly powerful. When you take the time to say goodbye to everyone you love, allowing yourself to feel everything that goes along with this final farewell, you appreciate your life a lot more. After finishing the letter, you can put those words in a safe place and go live your life in a way that makes them mean something. In the unforgettable words of Captain Miller (played by Tom Hanks in the Steven Spielberg film *Saving Private Ryan*), who has just sacrificed himself for a young private, "Earn this."

A death letter challenges you to be better now. You don't write it just on the contingency that you *might* die—because, of course, you will. That is guaranteed. This kind of letter allows you to focus on living a better life in the present. This practice of remembering death is what the Stoics called "memento mori," which they used to focus their awareness on living. Don't ever forget that the reaper is knocking at your door, waiting for your time. That's wisdom—knowing the inevitability of your demise and doing everything you can to make sure it's not in vain.

To live like we're dying means leaving nothing on the table. In terms of broken relationships, unresolved conflict, or unmet dreams and expectations, you have to be ready to die. Clean up the messes you made, fix what you broke, do your best. Facing death focuses us, as it should—not on our funeral and legacy but on the life we get to live now.

There's an old saying that my dad would tell me when I was in the military: "Putting on a uniform makes a soldier want to get married." It wasn't the uniform, mind you, nor was it something about the military specifically. He just meant that if you were going to die, you'd want to hold on to something living, like a wife and a few rug rats. A good warrior has a relish for life that exceeds that of the common man.

The military needs its soldiers ready to die. It needs them wholly focused on the mission ahead, not with unfinished business back home in the heat of battle. It's hard to think about flanking maneuvers under fire when your thoughts are hijacked by how you never forgave your dad or didn't propose to the girl you love. The point of a death letter is more than just saying nice things to the people you love. It's about enabling you to focus on the task at hand, giving it your full presence and attention.

You can't be all in on the project of the day if you failed to tell your children that you love them forever. Leaving nothing unsaid clears your mind of clutter so that you can be all in on the work in front of you. If you are reading carefully, you'll realize there's a piece of wisdom here that goes far beyond the soldier and lands squarely in your lap, but let's return again to the soldier.

To function best, a soldier needs a mind and soul unencumbered by broken relationships, hidden love, and withheld forgiveness. He needs to have sorted out the most critical issues regarding truth, meaning, and life. When he faces death now on the blank page of his own death letter, he is ready to die in the most practical of ways, making sure everything back home is taken care of; all affairs in order. In doing this, though, there is a fortunate by-product: he sees what is worth living for.

In a sense, a death letter is a sort of reverse bucket list, including all the things you already have and appreciate, giving you perspective on what you love the most and is worth your concern. Whatever doesn't make it into the letter is likely not worth your energy and can be cut from your life, or at least minimized. If it's not in the letter, then it's not worth dying (or living) for.

THE DANGER OF NOT DYING NOW

Why is it we rarely accomplish the dreams of childhood? Many of us never even got around to trying. And now, as death becomes more of a reality for many of us as we get older, we realize there is more road behind us than ahead. To my own surprise, I find myself in the middle of my life. I'm not a young man anymore, nor am I exactly "old." At best, my life is half over; at worst, I will die today. Am I ready for when that moment comes?

We all know our end will arrive, eventually. This should wake us up a little to what we have not yet done. Perhaps we still haven't made the impact we know we are capable of. Maybe there is a project we've delayed starting or a hard decision we keep avoiding. The closeness of death is a haunting thought but remains the unblinking reality in front of us all. If we haven't been living well, how can we expect to die well?

Facing your own death is one of the best experiences a man can have. Think of the hypochondriac who is so afraid of dying that he never really engages with life. To paraphrase the semifictional words of William Wallace, "all men die, but not all men truly live." If you haven't learned this firsthand, I'd encourage you to muster all your creative forces to learn it as quickly as possible before it's too late. The soldier knows how to live, because he knows how to die. Do you?

When we don't face death ahead of time, we end up living reactionary lives, drifting along the path of least resistance. We choose what's easy and comfortable over what's fulfilling and meaningful. We log hours, days, and years like this, asleep at the wheel. We may imagine that we'll grind out a living for just a little longer, then retire and really start living. But that line of thinking is a trap. Your life is right now. There isn't a "later." And how often do we make such promises to ourselves only to be surprised when a sudden tragedy or some surprise disease reminds us how foolish our plans were?

I see lots of people living like this, pining for a future that never comes, delaying what matters for later. You may find yourself in such a state now, whiling away the days in hopes of a better tomorrow. Telling yourself that you'll start living the way you know you should . . . after *this*. The next thing could be a raise, some stressful situation at home, or even a big goal. Then, you tell yourself, you'll spend more time with the kids and wife and focus on reconnecting with those you care most about. I don't have to tell you that this rarely, if ever, happens.

Sometimes, we are visited by an unexpected, and seemingly tragic, grace. A loved one dies. A close friend whose life is riddled with discontentment goes through a midlife crisis. You have a near-death experience or narrowly avoid disaster. Whatever the situation, something inside you wakes up and you realize how sweet life is and how much you were missing. These experiences don't have to be dramatic; they happen in subtle, everyday ways for most of us. We just have to notice them. Your kids may remind you that you're on your phone too much; the love of your life might tell you that you're coming home later each and every night. Whatever the case, there are wake-up calls everywhere, all telling us the same thing: the clock is ticking, and every moment matters.

SMILING AT DEATH

One of the worst things that was ever said to me was when I was preparing for a combat mission. We were doing our pre-mission checks, mentally going over the battle plan as per our recent operations order, and a buddy leaned over to me to say something to the effect of, "Man, I just got a bad feeling that you're not gonna make it."

And then—silence.

What was I supposed to do with that!? It was such a horrifically terrible thing to say to a person that it was, well, kind of funny. Just another classic moment of Ranger graveyard humor. Most wouldn't find it funny, of course, but most people aren't soldiers in Special Operations. Cops get this joke, as do paramedics, firefighters, and anyone who works in a very dangerous profession. We all lift an eyebrow and smile because it is just so heinously inappropriate. Surprisingly, this kind of humor helps us get through it, the kind of obnoxious thing brothers might do to each other that looks hateful but is anything but.

Good soldiers know to not take death too seriously, to not give it the benefit of respect. They joke about it, make fun of it, regularly bring it up in everyday conversation. To people on the outside, this sort of behavior may appear insensitive and disrespectful, even crass. But a dark sense of humor carries with it an important message: if you are able to laugh, it means you're still alive. Graveyard humor helps men weather the storms of life and reminds us that we're here . . . for now.

Laughing at death infuses levity into every aspect of life, including the darker parts. It teaches us flexibility in regard to the things we cannot control. Consider the difference between the branches of an oak tree, which will shatter into smithereens given enough wind, ice, and time; then contrast that with the limberness of a willow, which moves *with* the wind. The willow is no less strong but instead of refusing to bend until it breaks, it flexes with the wind. That's graveyard humor—a willingness to move with the challenges of life, even with death itself, and not take things so seriously.

Some things in life are so horrible that if you didn't have a certain flexibility (much in the way of comedy), then you're going to snap. You'll split in two, cracking like the tree that couldn't bend with the unpredictability of nature. Many of the most dangerous people on the planet have this kind of humor. They have to. We all do. Graveyard humor is a secret coping mechanism that when used correctly can get you through some of the worst times in your life. Facing death before we die takes away some of the fear. Sometimes, we can even learn to laugh at death. This is how you know you're really living: when you can stare into the abyss and smile.

HAVE YOU LIVED GREATLY?

Culturally, we don't like to talk about any of this. When someone dies, we talk *around* the fact of their death with euphemistic terms like "she passed away" or "they're gone." We don't want to know much outside of "Did they suffer?" We'd rather avoid the seemingly unnecessary details about their dying. Because, after all, they're gone, so why does it matter? But I think it *does* matter, and I want to know exactly how a person died. How you died tells me a lot about how well you lived.

Think of someone in your life who died not too long ago. Did they rejoice at the end? Did their lives matter? Did they leave life with a smile or frown? My personal hero died at the youthful age of thirty-three. Sure, he accomplished a bit more than me (saved mankind from their sins, rose from the dead, and founded the world's largest religion, for starters), but he also died with compassion for the very people who murdered him. I know I'm not close to that kind of goodness, but I hope to draw closer in the years ahead.

Another hero I've already mentioned is William Wallace. As legend has it, he was ripped to pieces at his execution. This was considered a heinous and shameful way to die, yet his followers were emboldened rather than disheartened by such a grotesque act.

Similarly, the early Christians were tortured to death for what they believed. The catacombs in Italy are lined with millions of underground graves, hundreds of thousands who were butchered for their convictions. The Roman Empire, in all its power, sought to destroy the early church, but the more Christians who were killed, the more rose in their place.

Tertullian wrote that the "blood of the martyrs is the seed of the Church," and that was certainly true back then. These were real people who believed something so strongly that they sealed it with their own blood. I don't care who you are or what you believe—that's pretty hard core. What outrageous strength and sacrifice! Death did not scare them, because their life was about so much more.

Even more shocking still was the way they died. Young women would sing gentle hymns while lions were being released to devour them. Newlyweds rejoiced that they would meet again one day before being skinned alive. Young men celebrated their passage from one life to the next, as flames were lit at their feet, soon burning them to ash. These people died well, because they were living for something greater than themselves.

The apostle Paul said, "To live is Christ and to die is gain." In the Bible, this early church leader was torn between two conflicting ideas: Go to heaven and be with Jesus or stay here on Earth, where there is pain and suffering and persecution? Because He'd found a mission bigger than His own life, He wrote (in my own little paraphrase): "Well, no, I'd rather die and go be with Jesus, duh." His life's purpose made death easy, even preferable; but it also clarified His time on Earth. Until that final day, which He considered a gift, He would live His life in accordance with the truth as best He could. When you serve something bigger than yourself, death loses its sting. What matters most is your mission, not how long you get to live it out. So you welcome your end, because in a way it is a familiar presence. It *will* happen, and when it does, you'll be ready.

At the time of writing this, I am thirty-nine years old. I have two young boys and a wife I want to love to a ripe old age. But let's suppose my time is up. Can I greet death with a smile? Do I possess the inner joy necessary to die with dignity? Have I made my time count? On a good day, the answer is . . . *maybe.* And this challenges me. Have you lived well enough that you would be ready to die right now? It's not a fun question, but it is the most sobering one you may have to answer.

There's a poem by Dylan Thomas that I find moving, in which he repeats over and over again: "Rage, rage against the dying of the light." At first, I'm inspired by the gritty, long-suffering spirit of the verse. But I'm also struck with empathy for the speaker who is imploring his audience, calling them to rage against the dying light. In the poem, you can see the shattered hopes, unmet goals, and the tragedy of a wasted life he is calling his listeners to rage against. I love and hate this. While my heart is still beating, I also want to rage—but not for purposeless existence, instead for what truly matters. I want to rage for love, for meaning, and for truth. When I pass, let me go gently into that good night: fulfilled and looking to greener pastures, knowing my time here was not a waste. I want to die with peace in my heart and not a tempest, and I believe this is possible for all of us.

A SOBER RESOLUTION

It is not enough to merely consider death and say your goodbyes now. You have to really relish life, living for more than a temporal existence. We need deep purpose to find meaning in our daily lives and be able to greet death with open arms. Suffice to say, not everyone does this, because it requires intentionality and, I daresay, faith.

In the book *The Question of God*, the Harvard professor Armand Nicholi compares the lives, legacies, and deaths of two men: Sigmund Freud and C. S. Lewis. Both men were considered great in their time, and their greatness multiplied exponentially after their deaths. Although they both deserve respect for their brilliant contributions to the world, I would only don Lewis with the title of Warrior Poet. Certainly, each man was brilliant; but only one died well.

Consider the following from Nicholi's book: "To fully live," he writes, "one must resolve the problem of death. When left unresolved, one spends excessive energy denying it or becoming obsessed with it." Freud became obsessed with death, dreaming about it constantly. His physician described this preoccupation as "superstitious and obsessive." After his sixtieth birthday, Freud wrote, "If I had known how little joy I would have on my sixtieth birthday, my first would probably not have given me pleasure, either. It would be in the best of times only a melancholic celebration." He died by euthanasia in 1939, telling his doctor that living was "nothing but torture and [it] makes no sense anymore."

Lewis, in stark contrast, reveals his thoughts in a letter not long before his death. "There are better things ahead," he wrote, "than any we leave behind. . . . Don't you think our Lord says to you, 'Peace, child, peace. Relax. Let go. Underneath are the everlasting arms. . . . Do you trust me so little?'" Not long after this letter, he slipped into a coma caused by a heart attack, only to recover for a few months afterward. During that time, Lewis was reported to be quite cheerful, calm, and filled with an inner peace. He wrote that he wished he had died from his heart attack since he had been so close to heaven's gate, then he went on to joke about how poor Lazarus was brought back and robbed of heaven's embrace.

Lewis's brother Warren gives us insight into his brother's final moments: "About a week before his death he said to me, 'I have done all that I was sent into the world to do, and I am ready to go.' I have never seen death looked in the face so tranquilly"

If you don't consider first what kind of death you will have, know for sure that you will not land accidentally on the life you want to live. For my part, I would like to have moved the souls of men during my time on this Earth. I would like my children's children around me at my deathbed, if at all possible. I want to see the bride of my youth standing over me, smiling, as if to say, "I'll see you again soon." I would like to have no apologies when I pass to the next life. No unfinished business. I want to go silently, with a smile, into that good night. No raging necessary. That is my ideal, and I know I'm nowhere close to it, but the finish line must be established before the race can begin. Only when we decide how we want to die can we begin to really live.

I'll close this chapter with a short poem I wrote about life and death titled, "Hurry! Hurry!":

Hurry! Hurry!
Life calls! An urgent schedule awaits!
Today I will catch up, or better still . . . plow ahead.
For I have my tasks and my tasks have me.
And I will find out only too late
that beyond the noise lies peace.
For there is beauty without.
There is majesty above.
And hallowed ground is underfoot.
And my thirsty soul yawns within.

—JOHN LOVELL

PRACTICUM

Write your death letter.

This is not a thought experiment. Really do it. There will come a day when you are no longer here, and you'll want your friends and family to know what you thought of them. Don't go to the next chapter until you've spent some time with this. If you let it, it'll transform you.

Take some time, at least an hour if you can spare it, and really think through who you'd want to make sure is taken care of, what you want looked after, and how you'd speak to those you love.

As you write these words, take note of how you feel and what it does to your perspective.

Say your final words on those pages, seal them up, then tell someone where to find them if something happens to you. Before you can live fully, you have to face death, and writing this letter is a great way to sort out what your priorities are.

It's time to live like you are dying.

5

The War of Ideas

The society that separates its scholars from its warriors will have its thinking done by cowards and its fighting done by fools.

—THUCYDIDES

I n college, I took a philosophy course that bothers me to this day. In retrospect, though, I don't think it was the class but the person teaching it. My professor was in her midfifties and wore thick, oversize glasses on a round and jovial face. I liked her at first, but that didn't last long.

Each day, she would introduce the class to a different philosopher from the past and detail the outlines of what they believed. I ate this stuff up. We students would then wrestle with those particular beliefs, and she would spar against us. All good so far, right? That's what good educators do, I think. But here's where my big beef came in.

Much later in the semester, I observed a shift happening in my fellow students. They came into the class with some strong notions of what they thought to be true but ended the class believing in almost no concepts of truth at all. Two plus two didn't equal four anymore. Instead, four became a concept that may be true for some and not for others; and by the way, what is "truth," anyway, and why on earth does it matter? I felt like they all were going mad.

It started to bother me immensely that our professor seemed intent on destroying the students' concepts of truth. She wasn't sparring with us to make us better; rather, she was like a grown adult walking through a kids' martial arts class distributing haymakers and dropkicks. It felt more like child abuse than productive coaching. Never did she offer better truths in the place of what was being undermined.

It's one thing to disagree with another person's worldview, to call it into question and hopefully learn from the debate, but it's quite another to dismantle the very notion that truth is a reality at all. It seemed our teacher wanted to make sure no one put together a cohesive worldview, and that was simply unacceptable to me. That, after all, is the *point* of philosophy. But in opposing this progress, she became not a philosopher, but an antiphilosopher. A destroyer of truth. A postmodern deconstructionist.

This was my first brush with this kind of pseudo-academic, and I found her approach to be a pernicious poison.

Our current era is marked by an ideological war on anything traditional. In a so-called search for progress, cultural deconstructionists have led our country's young minds to believe they can make up whatever truth they want without question. Truth is now considered relative, and we are all free to believe whatever we want. Which is just a way of saying the truth no longer exists. But this belief is dangerous and not without consequence. The moment we believe it, true philosophy is dead, and that simply cannot be.

How could a philosopher *not* fight to find truth and live by those precepts? How could they stay silent when others were searching beside them? The Greeks had to literally kill Socrates to shut him up. Yes, his questions tore down, but they also had a way of building up. He was trying to clear the chaff in order to have healthy and real beliefs.

Whether you consider yourself a philosophical person or not, you very likely have a view of the world that you believe is true. A willingness to defend that truth and stand up for what you believe to be right is an essential practice of every Warrior Poet. Our greatest weapon is not our hands but our minds, and the sooner we learn to use logic and reason to outthink our adversaries, the better world we can build. And lest you think I am advocating that we all start donning berets and using words like "epistemological," bear with me as I unpack what a modern-day philosopher looks like.

WHY TRUTH MATTERS

I know the word "philosophy" likely conjures images of old dudes dressed in waistcoats, sitting in wingback chairs while they smoke their pipes with nothing better to do than contemplate the mysteries of existence. But philosophy isn't reserved for just the academics. It has to do with how we see the world and what it all means. Good philosophy may sometimes start in the clouds but it should end in the dirt—in the everyday, practical way we go through life.

The word "philosophy" literally means the "love of wisdom." A philosopher is a person who loves what is true and what is rational. Furthermore, I'd say that philosophy is how science, history, experience, and so on form the very basis of our lives. In other words, it's how all the pieces fit together to form a holistic view of how the world works. All the individual pieces of knowledge connect to one another through the highways of philosophy. This means that we need philosophy to make sense of the world around us, and then we can figure out our place in it.

Everyone is constantly building and editing their philosophy of the world; it cannot be helped. The big questions for us, though, are: How good of a job are we doing? Have we gotten the most important stuff right? Does our worldview fit well together so that our theology fits well with our politics, the history of the world, and the sciences? If there is a contradiction, then there's a misstep somewhere and we must back up and revise some or all of what we think we know. I believe a philosophical system must be cohesive, true, and actually work. If your philosophy of marriage brings about an 85 percent divorce rate, I'd say your philosophy of marriage sucks and you should find something that not only seems rational but actually works.

Everyone's got a philosophy, but some are clearly better than others. A good philosophy leads to greater understanding and it builds more and more so we can know more and more and make better decisions. A bad philosophy, at the very least, doesn't make sense and creates more confusion. Sometimes, a truly terrible philosophy can lead to all kinds of atrocities and disaster, too, so all of us have a stake in the game of calling out bad philosophies. Consider that Mother Teresa had a philosophy of living, as did Mao Zedong and Pol Pot. So, what we believe affects how we live, and this is what we mean by the word "philosophy."

It pains me to say it, but I think many of our modern intellectuals are destroyers of truth. They're not making the pieces of reality fit into coherent explanations; instead, they're turning them into confetti. The aim of these so-called teachers isn't to build on what we already know but to destroy ancient wisdom simply because it is ancient. A true philosopher, on the other hand, seeks a universal understanding of the world that applies to the whole human experience.

I know this isn't agreeable to our postmodern ears, but outside the last fifty or so years, this was the goal of all philosophy: to connect the dots of human understanding in a system of thought that makes sense. Our world depends on such a love for wisdom as well as our willingness to fight for it. Whether we realize it or not, we still need philosophy—in fact, now more than ever.

I'm part of what sociologists call the "millennial generation." Our parents were either boomers or Gen Xers, and our children are Gen Zers. Millennials have some solid qualities, but, oh man, do we harbor some terrible flaws. Philosophically, we seem to be largely oblivious. Unless you were homeschooled, you probably never had a logic or rhetoric class or anything to do with philosophy until midway through college—which is way too late of a start, in my opinion.

Philosophy is the subject all other disciplines have to go through to arrive at themselves. You can't do science without a philosophy of science. You can't do history without a philosophy of history. I have since realized that my former professor was at best a "history of philosophy" professor and not an actual philosopher.

While real philosophers seek to better understand what is true and live by it, anti-philosophers want to argue there are no absolute truths and that everything is merely relative. This is not how philosophers thought for thousands of years and it's important to take a moment now to figure out how in the world we got to where we are by examining the past. As Orwell points out, "Who controls the past controls the future." So if we want to unravel what's happening here and now, we have to visit our philosophical past.

HOW WE GOT HERE

From the first through the sixteenth century, the philosophical system for the Western world was built in harmony with a theological understanding that basically boiled down to "God says." For much of modern human history, that simple phrase defined the center of truth. Why are there clouds in the sky? Why does the sun rise and set at the same time every day? Where did we come from and where are we going? It all came back to a theological understanding of the world that centered around an all-good, all-powerful creator.

From the sixteenth through the eighteenth century, however, a new era of thought was born. The Age of Enlightenment marked a transition in human history away from the religious presuppositions of the past and moved toward reason. It was a time of intellectual rebirth, scientific discovery, and philosophical inquiry. This was an era when people chose to follow reason as well as God, and many welcomed such changes in the name of progress. Wanting to throw off the shackles of superstitious thinking, which in their defense could be quite bloody, these generations of men and women let reason be their guide and logic their god.

The Enlightenment, though a raging success in some areas, was largely a philosophical failure. For the better part of human history up until that time, man derived truth from revelation. During the Age of Enlightenment, however, revelation no longer dictated the underpinnings of how we understood truth.

Reason alone would fill that gap. This was not a bad thing in that faith and reason are meant to go hand in hand; but faith without reason is not faith, and reason without faith cannot give us morality, meaning, nor hope.

The problem with the Enlightenment was the proverbial throwing the baby out with the bathwater. Reason by itself cannot answer the most important questions of the human heart. If God has not spoken and faith is a sham, then on what should we base our concepts of right and wrong?

Without some universal standard for what is true and good, what we believe is just made up. It isn't transcendent. Using this line of reasoning, we can make a moral system that says rape, murder, and racism are wrong, then later say it's all okay—and who is anyone to judge? After all, how can you say racism is wrong when it's an arbitrary judgment of popular or individual opinion? Do you see the problem? If there is no moral lawgiver, then there is no real moral law other than what we humans make up.

A literary hero who embodied Enlightenment ideals was Sherlock Holmes: a man driven by his unparalleled intellect and compulsion to fix unsolvable problems. With his genius as his primary resource, Sherlock found great success and was rewarded for it. He was also a pretty miserable guy. This was an astute creative choice by Sir Arthur Conan Doyle, the author who created Holmes. That kind of a man, the kind who is left only to his own intelligence and self-determination, would be quite miserable.

The human machine runs on more than logic. We are hungry for purpose, meaning, love, free will, and moral causes. It turns out there is more to life than rationality, and there's something beyond this physical world that cannot be examined under a microscope. Failure to ignore these things empties the joy out of a person and ignores truths we know intuitively in the deeper parts of our being. Living as the naturalist does forces us to erase so many of the things that make life full and worth living. Our philosophical system should encompass reason, but it must also include the fullness of the human condition and being. Of course Sherlock was miserable. He was a man living as a soulless machine.

Sherlock Holmes is the perfect expression of what a life experienced in the mind can do to a man. It is not enough. Like the Tin Man—like all men—this man needs a heart, and that is the role of the poet in our world today, the true philosopher who points us back to truth and transcendent meaning. We simply cannot thrive without it.

The human spirit is not a machine that can survive on mere facts. We need something more than the glorification of ourselves and intellects. We need a truth bigger than our brains can conceive. All men, in my experience, long for purpose. We need to believe there is a point to our suffering and a reason for otherwise inexplicable pain. We want something to love and hope it loves us back, to know that we aren't alone in this world. This is something the existentialists rightly caught on to that the rationalists and empiricists failed to fully appreciate.

The modern era, however, is a time when people have grown accustomed to picking and choosing what they want to be true. As soon as a certain philosophy stops serving us, we discard it for whatever is preferable. But we can't build a model of meaning for the universe with just logic. The great thinkers of old realized full and well that reason couldn't be mankind's sole guide. The Enlightenment thinkers pushed God out of the center of wisdom and inserted reason in His place, but the substitute did not satisfy the hearts of men.

The twentieth century was a time rife with experimentation in thinking and expression. All of it was intended to create a reaction, to attempt to answer our deepest questions of meaning with simply more questions. Somehow, this was meant to pull all the pieces together, which was not altogether wrong but still lacking.

Expressions of truth are important to understanding reality, but they are only expressions of a deeper reality. The modern era failed to produce a robust and consistent philosophy. We went from "God says . . ." before the Enlightenment, to "Reason says . . ." during the Enlightenment, and then to "What is truth?" in the modern area. Now, we've arrived at the worst place yet. Postmodernism claims, "Truth is whatever you decide it is." It becomes relative, as does morality and any basis for goodness. When you believe something is true and somebody else believes something antithetical to that, and somehow you're both right, well, that's ridiculous. This is not putting the pieces together but scattering them around in some twisted display of rebellion. Anti-philosophers have parted company with the philosophers of old and with one stroke have erased all concrete truth. I believe the effects of this will play out over decades to destroy the fabric of society, something that has already been happening at a quickening pace.

By and large, the younger generations do not believe in any absolute truth. Something simple as "two plus two equals four" is now an idea, not a reality. *That's your truth*, someone might object, *but to me, two plus two equals five.* This type of thinking is obviously dangerous but is becoming the norm. It's going to take courage to stand up to such anti-philosophy that has gained traction before it dismantles the very system on which our world was built. Those who argue such a position will immediately contradict themselves. Let's have their employer add their paycheck up wrong and see how quickly they can add two and two to make four. In the end, we all want a universal truth, at least when it clearly benefits us.

A WAR OF IDEAS

The state of the world is not just a product of how people have acted throughout history. It is also a product of how we think. Now, more than ever, the conflicts in which we engage require not just fists and firearms but wits. We Warrior Poets must do more than fight. We must grow in knowledge and wisdom. As

John Steinbeck wrote, "The final weapon is the brain, all else is supplemental."

These days, many people seem to have a bleak view of where the world is headed, and I confess to being one of them. How can we expect our country to stand after postmodern philosophy has destroyed its foundations?

America was built on concrete ideals and absolute truths of natural laws and freedoms. But what happens when these truths are regarded as relative instead? What happens when young minds regard our ideals as no more valid than someone else's truth? When our capitalist markets are replaced by government-controlled ones, as many young people now seem grossly and naively in favor of? When this happens, we are, indeed, in great peril. When we are no longer "one nation under God" and are denied "life, liberty, and the pursuit of happiness," we may soon long for something so "regressive" as universal truth.

And what if we come to this realization far too late?

We all have a responsibility to know and defend the truth, to become good philosophers in our own right. Not long ago, I came across a story in a book by the great G. K. Chesterton, who was known for possessing a very eccentric kind of genius. Here's what he wrote:

> *Suppose that a great commotion arises in the street about something, let us say a lamp-post, which many influential persons desire to pull down. A gray-clad monk, who is the spirit of the Middle Ages, is approached upon the*

matter, and begins to say, in the arid manner of the School-men, "Let us first of all consider, my brethren, the value of Light. If Light be in itself good—" At this point he is somewhat excusably knocked down. All the people make a rush for the lamp-post, the lamp-post is down in ten minutes, and they go about congratulating each other on their medieval practicality. But as things go on they do not work out so easily. Some people have pulled the lamp-post down because they wanted the electric light; some because they wanted old iron; some because they wanted darkness, because their deeds were evil. Some thought it not enough of a lamp-post, some too much; some acted because they wanted to smash municipal machinery; some because they wanted to smash something. And there is war in the night, no man knowing whom he strikes. So, gradually and inevitably, to-day, to-morrow, or the next day, there comes back the conviction that the monk was right after all, and that all depends on what is the philosophy of Light. Only what we might have discussed under the gas-lamp, we now must discuss in the dark.

You and I may believe different things, but just because we don't agree on what is true doesn't mean there isn't some universal standard of truth out there. The aim of philosophy is to find that, or at least get closer to it. This is a good pursuit, even if it's a bit maddening at times. We all want some standard on which to base our lives, even if we don't admit it.

Folks who think truth is relative can't possibly live consistently with such a belief; and as far as I can tell, they don't try. We all believe in some form of absolute truth, at least when it affects what matters most to us.

Relativists stand on the framework of a world of absolute truths while commanding their own private truths. It doesn't work like that. Mind you, I'm not talking about your *perspective* on truth, which remains yours and yours alone. I'm talking about absolute truths that are true whether you and I agree on them or not. These are like the laws of science and math. Some things just are, and this should not be as extreme of a viewpoint as it is currently considered to be.

THE COST OF LIES

Whether we realize it or not, we are being told exactly what we should believe every day. When we express our ideas in a way that is not congruent with the whims of culture, we may be shamed, cast out, attacked, or even silenced. Cancel culture is not just a bully; it's authoritarianism disguised as "progress."

In America, we have the wonderful gift of freedom of speech, at least for now. I can say my ideas, regardless of how horrible they sound to you, and you can say yours, and the government is not allowed to shut either of our viewpoints down. That's a good thing. That's freedom. It doesn't exist in China where you cannot criticize your leaders. It doesn't exist in many Muslim countries where you are not legally allowed to carry or own a Bible.

We can discuss what we believe and fight over our own understandings of truth, and this is all very good. The ability to believe whatever we want is a right—one we should fight to protect. To disagree without worrying about our safety is something we should not take for granted. This is what is at stake when we consider the place of truth in the world today. We must believe in some universal, objective reality by which we measure everything. We may not know exactly what it is, but having some sort of basis allows us to grow in wisdom and understanding.

Through dialogue and disagreement, we all have the opportunity to learn from one another and get closer to what is true. This requires a certain amount of maturity and humility on our parts. We have to be open to the possibility that we might be wrong and that deeper truths are at least possible.

These days, though, I am afraid, our kids are more familiar with microaggressions, safe spaces, and hate speech. They know that if someone offends them with an idea they don't like, they have carte blanche to vent limitless rage on them. This is not okay. We have to learn to love wisdom again, start earnestly seeking truth, and be open to opinions that are unattractive to us.

I was open to relative truth until I weighed it and dismissed it as self-defeating lunacy. Though we ought to be open-minded, it's not a forever kind of open-mindedness. I'm not open-minded to selling kids into slavery. I'm not open-minded to lynching people who look different than I do. "The point of a mind,"

Chesterton says, "is the same as an open mouth. It's meant to close on something solid."

These are the precepts on which America was built—universal truths and laws that are worth debating and reconsidering but ultimately held as important ideals. Our Founding Fathers understood that these beliefs were not just givens; they would have to be fought for and defended, sometimes with bloody consequence. The truth was so important that men were willing to die for it. We pretend that today we're too civilized for such seemingly barbarian values, that our nature has somehow changed, but this is an illusion.

Those of us in the United States sit protected by vast oceans and the greatest military the world has ever seen. We enjoy immense prosperity and delude ourselves into thinking our current situation will last forever. When the ideas upon which our culture was founded are called into question, as they currently are, our very way of life is threatened. Though you may feel protected well enough now, there is an incredible cost to discarding what we've previously understood as truth for no good reason other than it's old.

The war for ideas has real consequences. Hitler argued for eugenics and a cleansing of the gene pool. He shut down the intellectual class who might challenge him, took guns away from the people so they could not resist him, set up a police state with sophisticated surveillance, then murdered more than six million Jews in concentration camps. Today, our Big Tech oligarchy censors pro-life social media accounts to give free rein to abortion advocates. The media and universities work hard to present a one-sided argument to the world. The game is rigged and the results are tragic.

America, however, is waking up. A fog of propaganda is lifting, and people are standing up for those who cannot yet stand. We must not fail to put forth our arguments in this crucial conflict. Vote, speak, argue, write, report, film, and sing the truth; through arts and sciences, politics and culture, we must work to retake our institutions of power and break free of the postmodernists. We cannot rest until justice and truth are once again honored.

DEFENDING THE TRUTH

What we have now in our culture is a crippling poison that is internally weakening us while forces around us grow stronger. Our soldiers exist to deploy around the globe in the interest of defending our freedom. But that fight is happening here on home soil, too; it's just happening on ideological grounds.

The battle for the mind is where we will win or lose this next season of humanity. And right now, the cause for truth seems to be taking a major hit, with the most damning of all blows to how public discourse is breaking down.

Have you noticed how everyone is just ticked off all the time? Progressives seem to look around and see fence posts erected by tradition, and in their rage against the wisdom of the past, they seek to tear down any boundaries or limitations they see—even ones that may be good for us. But you can't tear down a fence post until you understand why it was put up in the first place.

Otherwise, you are doing what my professor did: playing with truth as if it were a lump of putty to be molded into whatever shape you'd like. That's not how truth works, and that's not how reality works. If you mess with the laws of the universe enough, eventually there's a correction. And it is often not very pretty or gentle.

What we seem to be aiming for now is the destruction of the past by categorically rejecting all tradition. There is a difference between saying our parents got *some* things wrong and saying they got *everything* wrong. Our culture is now waging war on every type of authority, on everything in the past, including every tradition whatsoever. And that's going too far.

Honestly, I can't believe that I, a barely-middle-aged dude who used to hang out with skateboard punks, have become such a ranting curmudgeon! But it's all this craziness that's pushed me to say, "All right maybe Mom and Dad weren't completely wrong. Maybe our grandparents and parents, our forebears, actually had some really good points." Look at the marriages of our great-grandparents compared to those from more recent generations and you can immediately surmise that they understood some stuff we simply don't. Namely, commitment, fidelity, and honor. Why is it so crazy to consider that something new is not always necessarily better?

All of this reminds me of a George Orwell quote from *1984*. Now, this book was written many decades ago, but it's written in a way that you'd think it had just been published, considering how it addresses the social atmosphere of its time. "Every record has been destroyed or falsified," Orwell writes, "every book rewritten, every picture has been repainted, every statue and street building has been renamed, every date has been altered. And the process is continuing day by day and minute by minute. History has stopped. Nothing exists except an endless present in which the Party is always right."

The quote nails the landscape of today more than ever before, because it illustrates an ideology that is prevalent, one that its adherents will use to tear down and destroy all evidence of the past, to eradicate anything that attempts to look back in history. The truth of previous generations is being removed and rewritten, and all that exists is the ideological party now.

When you've destroyed the past, you can create the future, making it into whatever you want. When truth is subjective and we have no collective history, the systems of power will tell us what is true and where we come from. In other words, it's exactly what an authoritarian government would want its people to believe, because they will be easy to control. You've heard the old adage, "If you don't stand for something, you'll fall for anything!" This is a problem for any freedom-loving human.

The propagandists had our statues taken down. They rioted and marched and demanded that we paper over where we came from. As Orwell wrote, "The most effective way to destroy people is to deny and obliterate their own understanding of their history." Today, history is being rewritten before our very eyes, and many people are letting it happen. But this works only when individuals are compliant with corrupt systems that love power over truth. The Warrior Poet will not stand for such dishonesty and oppression. The buck stops with us.

Now for some good news (since I know it was getting pretty heavy there for a while): I see a class of men and women standing up and defying the status quo, declaring war on the destruction of everything. We freedom fighters must rally together, as fellow poets striving to be forces for good in a world, using our voices to defend the truth. You and I are those who are called to stand up for what is right and good. Our job is not to defend tradition for the sake of itself, but to protect our heritage so that we have something to build upon. To tear down the very structures of society just because they are old and seemingly outdated is not progress; it's anarchy. We will invariably repeat the mistakes of the past, and those could very well be deadly.

It really does start with us. Our actions must create the tide that raises all other ships. As individuals, we have the capacity for corruption and often choose it but are shocked when our governments mirror the same such corruption. The opposite can happen, as well. We can be better men. We can learn to love truth and wisdom. When enough little lights grow into a mighty flame, we can be a beacon for good in a world that has lost its mind. But we're going to have to get tough and bold and understand that such a stand will cost us something personally. But it will be worth it.

ARM YOURSELF WITH INFORMATION

It's been said, "He who doesn't read the newspapers isn't uninformed. He who reads the newspapers is misinformed." Everything these days is getting eaten up by politics, so whatever becomes a political conversation is now politics; and it's erased our ability to talk about anything but the weather. Oh wait! *Climate change!* I forgot. We can't even talk about the weather anymore without having to pick sides and draw party lines.

Personally, I'm always having to choose between getting bad information and no information at all. More often than not, I choose the lesser of two evils: to be informed even if it means that it comes from a biased source. We must be discerning in what information we take in and what "news" we choose to believe. The soldier needs to be pure in his cause, ready to fight for something he emphatically believes in. This is the truth we must be ready to die for.

In that sense, every warrior is a philosopher, a poet of sorts, because the poet doesn't just think about truth—he defends it with words and action. We've got to have the will to fight, especially with our minds. Any boy can play war. A real man understands the strategy of the enemy and is aware of all fronts on which he is attacking. Every war is fought both on the battlefield and in the mind. This is why the Nazis spread all kinds of anti-Jewish and anti-American propaganda during World War II; they understood that psychology was as important as military technology. This has not changed. Our enemy is alive and well, hitting us from all fronts, including education and information. We must be ready to ward off such attacks, to fight for the truth and defend it at all costs.

If we don't have that will to fight, then our warrior ethos is more of a hobby than a calling. It's not easy to fight any battle, including one of ideas. Because when the inevitable fear and chaos come, you won't be able to conjure up that fighter mindset, ready to suffer for the truths you hold dear. Not unless you're trained to do so.

So we gotta get this stuff right, and we gotta do it now.

MAKE WAR WITH IGNORANCE

Socrates was more than one of the greatest minds of the ancient world. In his youth, the brilliant philosopher-to-be stacked bodies with the great warriors of Athens. His protégé, Plato, tells us that Socrates was an infantryman and participated in three different military campaigns during the Peloponnesian War. Far from a mere foot soldier, he stood out as one of the most ferocious and fearless of men of his time.

In one story, we are told of an incident when the Athenian general Alcibiades was wounded and caught ahead of the defensive line—beyond where he could be protected by his fellow countrymen. Seeing his beloved war captain about to be killed, Socrates broke ranks and rushed to defend him, single-handedly slashing wildly at enemies closing in around him with no concern for his own safety. This heroic display moved the men to push the line forward and rescue their fallen captain.

The story of Socrates's death is more heroic than his war stories, even a little haunting. I think about it every time I hear the word "philosopher." The father of Western philosophy was killed for seeking the truth. The Athenian government knew ideas were dangerous and that this philosopher had a way of deconstructing all sorts of things people thought they knew. He was a questioner, but he wasn't messing with ideas for the sake of causing a ruckus. He was after *the* truth.

Socrates was aware of his own ignorance. As he grew in age and wisdom, he became incredibly competent at revealing the ignorance of other men—and that of governments. It was because the political powers felt threatened by this man and the fact that they could not shut him up, that they eventually put a choice before him. He could either face exile or drink poison and die.

The philosopher believed he'd be no better off in exile from his homeland than dead, which is what many great men who love their countries may believe. It would be better to die in accordance with the law of the land that he had upheld and defended his whole life than to abandon it for his own safety. Despite his friends begging their teacher to reconsider, Socrates drank to his own death and died. In a way, we all have to be willing to do this. To stand our ground for what we believe, fight physically to protect it, and sacrifice ourselves (perhaps literally, but more often socially) for the sake of the truth.

Philosophers run after what is true. They are deep and broad thinkers who consider all that is known and try to piece those ideas together in a worldview that makes sense. Socrates believed in truth and fought for it; he also was willing to acknowledge what he didn't know. A real philosopher lives and dies for this pursuit, never settling for what someone tells him is real. He wants reality itself, or as close to it as he can get.

Every good man must be a philosopher, a poet in the truest sense, and the problem with relative truth is that it is impossible to live by. You cannot die for the belief in nothing, cannot give up friendships and comfort for some amorphous idea that everyone is right, no matter what they believe.

This war of ideas is seen most visibly in the university system, but it's infecting all our educational institutions. College students, in particular, are racking up huge student loans to unlearn the most basic things even children know. It is astounding to me that someone can spend $100,000 on a master's degree and come out confused on the difference between boys and girls.

It doesn't stop with school. The American military has been hijacked into playing illogical woke games that only make us more vulnerable. As a former military man, I'll just come right out and say that you cannot build a strong and ferocious fighting force while demoralizing your soldiers with nonsensical notions of identity politics. A soldier must be fully resolved that his cause is a good one, one worth living and dying for. We should be arming our warriors with guns and courage, not "America is evil, racist, and xenophobic" messaging.

The Second Amendment to the U.S. Constitution immediately follows the First Amendment, because our Founding Fathers knew our rights would need protecting. In the First Amendment, we are given certain inalienable rights, including the right to freedom of speech, freedom of religion, and freedom of the press. These men understood that our freedoms were God-given rights but that they could easily be taken away. The Second Amendment secures our right to bear arms, which is meant to help us protect what we fought so hard to get. To be a Warrior Poet means understanding what rights and freedoms you've received from previous generations and being willing to fight to keep them.

PRACTICUM

Read a book, bro. Yes, you are technically reading a book now, so good job, but I'm really urging you toward a lifestyle of reading and continued education. It's the only way to stave off ignorance and deceit. I'll even make it easy and say audiobooks count (as long as you aren't doing something else while listening). Reading anything is a great start, but try to go deep. Read some classics—you know, those books you pretended to read in high school but didn't. If you need some authors to get you started, try out: Steven Pressfield, John Eldredge, Stephen Mansfield, C. S. Lewis, William Shakespeare, Victor Hugo, John Milton, George Orwell, and other names you've heard repeated over the years. Bonus points for reading the Bible. Becoming a lover of wisdom is not hard. There's so much good stuff out there. We just need to read it.

6

Every Warrior Needs a Muse

O, for a muse of fire that would ascend the brightest heaven of invention.

—WILLIAM SHAKESPEARE

R ebekah and I had been dating for two weeks, and we were standing on the back deck of a friend's house during a party when it happened. I don't remember what we were talking about, just that she was looking into my eyes and then, in a moment of sudden realization, drew back a step and said, "Oh, you've got it bad!"

This young woman I barely knew at this point offered an amused smile, turned on her heel, and rejoined the party, leaving me alone, vulnerable, and humiliated. *Did that just happen?* I wondered. *Did she really catch me falling in love with her and then, without reassuring me in any way that she felt the same, flit off to rejoin her friends?!*

Yes, I had completely fallen for this woman, and she not only knew it; she called me out on it! She didn't say, "Aw, I really like you, too!" Nope. She was terrible, but in a compelling and haunting way. It only made me want her more. She was enjoying the hunt and skipped off to let me continue my pursuit. *What kind of woman is this*, I wondered. I knew I should either quit the chase or marry her immediately. And, of course, it was really no choice at all. I had to make this woman my wife. She was right: I did, after all, have it bad.

As Warrior Poets, we are part of an ancient brotherhood of sworn protectors, and I am honored to be counted among such ranks. As I salute my brothers, however, I must admit that even this is not enough. Maybe my soul is greedy, but I'll contend yours is, too. There is a craving in all men that even an illustrious brotherhood cannot fill. We need something else, something soft and beautiful that quells the warrior spirit.

A man needs a muse.

AVOIDING A SHALLOW LIFE

Warrior Poets do not live for themselves. We live for a higher purpose. We are ready to defend the innocent and sacrifice ourselves on their behalf. We love our fellow man. We are freedom fighters. In these ideals, we find purpose and belonging. For us, it is not enough to merely indulge ourselves endlessly. All that pleasure eventually gets old, and you're left wondering, *What is this all about?* We need something more.

Blaise Pascal, a brilliant seventeenth-century mathematician and philosopher cuts right to the chase when he says, "What else does this craving, and this helplessness, proclaim but that there was once in man a true happiness, of which all that now remains is the empty print and trace? This he tries in vain to fill with everything around him, seeking in things that are not there the help he cannot find in those that are, though none can help, since this infinite abyss can be filled only with an infinite and immutable object; in other words by God himself."

Men need a purpose that is bigger than their own lives, however exciting they may seem at the time. We need a good reason to die, and the noble warrior is willing to sacrifice himself for a sacred calling. What we fight for is not why we fight. We may fight for our families or countries, but why we protect them must come from someplace deeper.

For me personally, I love my country, but patriotism is not the highest purpose that sustains me. I love my family, but what would happen to my purpose if my family were taken from me? I love my job, but this will not fulfill my need for belonging. Though each Warrior Poet can choose whatever purpose they live for, mine is not found in friends, hobbies, pleasure, or success. My purpose is to love and serve Jesus Christ with every ounce of my being. From this source comes a love for people, a motive for protecting them, as well as a deep and fulfilling worldview, not to mention the ground rules for all relationships.

The warrior needs more than war to live a happy life. So I ask: What are you living for? What will you fight for? Are you ever concerned that even as you fight, you could lose the reason you do it all? What then? We need a purpose, and that purpose must be bigger than ourselves or the love of our lives. The warrior is helped by a muse in their journey toward purpose, because she can serve as a means of drawing out who he really is as well as urging him to climb higher.

This is not the case when a relationship turns toxic or grows cold, but there is hope, because a relationship that can begin to wither can also be brought back to life. Your muse was worth fighting for initially, so they are worth fighting for now. Do the hard work of loving them even when you don't feel like it, even when you feel they don't "deserve" it. For even when looked at selfishly, it is by way of a muse that we reach further than we otherwise would have dared to go.

That day on the back deck, my wife-to-be was teaching a lesson that would be reinforced throughout our relationship. She is my constant reminder that life is more complex than I want it to be—that the point of the chase isn't necessarily to get what you're seeking, but to keep chasing. She also helps me understand what "relationship" means: an endless overflow of love and life.

That's what a muse does.

When Rebekah skipped away, I was in a complete daze, absolutely captivated. How did she do that? This was a power I hadn't seen before, and it frustrated me. I also couldn't get enough of it. She helped me find a depth to and a gusto for life that I couldn't access on my own, not entirely. A muse may not be a woman, per se, but it must be something or someone that calls you beyond yourself and into relationship.

Rebekah wants me to keep pursuing her, and this is a never-ending pursuit, which early on left me wondering, *What's the point?* Of course, the point is love. Love always grows and increases, seeking to multiply itself. But early on, this woman taught me to not give up so easily, to keep striving toward my purpose when it would be easier to quit. My purpose is to love God, and when I do that, I cannot help but love others, including my wife. We Warrior Poets fight for a purpose, and our muse keeps us rooted in it.

THE FALSE MUSES OF YOUTH

Growing up in the woods as a kid, I loved swimming in the lake and climbing trees. There was no thought to the future or what kind of man I should become. There was only *Play*, the one word that dominated my consciousness, and all the highs and lows that came with such a pursuit. I had the freedom to be independent and explore the woods beyond my home, roaming my neighborhood until it got dark. I spent hours and days on imagined adventures, largely unafraid and unfettered by the difficulties of life.

Later, my first social sphere was a bit of a skater, almost punkish group. If you're from the eighties, you might remember the

JNCO pants, the shaved-under skater haircut, and chain wallets. I might have been *that* kid for a while, but you must understand I would have given anything to be cool. *Play* had been supplanted, and *Cool* was on the throne. This didn't last long, though, until I sought the next way to belong.

When high school hit, I discovered wrestling. Really, I got picked out of the halls by a stocky wrestling coach who needed to fill the 103-pound spot. I was shrimpy enough to fill the lowest weight class while still remaining athletic enough to be ambulatory. Because there was no one else who volunteered, I made the team. In my first match, I was slaughtered, and I wish that was an exaggeration. It was a savage beating, and worse still, it happened in front of my mother, father, and grandmother. Some senior who could grow a goatee toyed with me for the entire match and pinned me in the last fifteen seconds. Imagine a cat playing with its food and finally killing it when the torture had left its prey nearly lifeless. You get the idea. Just so you know, it really sucks to be a mouse.

In that butchering, though, I discovered a new word to serve me. *Cool* was out, and *Winning* was in. I hated losing so much that I discovered a love for the chess of combat. It was such an all-encompassing test of strength, will, and skill that I fell in love with wrestling almost immediately. It's so odd that something that caused so much difficulty and pain could garner so much obsession and affection. But there you have it, yet another paradox of the masculine journey: discipline is freedom.

As I trained, I became a determined and gritty kind of kid,

developing a one-track mind obsessed with cutting weight and beating opponents. My confidence grew. I was taking the shape of something somewhat manly, but my yearning for meaning among unworthy muses was still developing. Playing, being cool, and winning, I found, were worthy inspirations for a while, but ultimately unsatisfactory. I needed something greater to chase after still.

I graduated and attended college, because it was the thing to do after high school, never even considering another option. In college, I parted company with my old flame *Winning* and found a new word to serve wholeheartedly: *Party*.

After joining a fraternity, I experienced a massive shift. The determined wrestler from high school got lost for a while. Please forgive me, reader, but I wore bow ties, danced the Carolina shag, and got hammered nearly every night of the week. I was not pausing in between crazy nights to wonder where the determined young man had gone. I didn't care to sit and construct a five-year plan, uninterested in plans past those of the evening. I had gotten older, but I was not unlike the child wandering the woods who thirsted to be cool and play all the time. I was adrift in my life and didn't know how or where to find a solid foothold. I needed a muse who wouldn't let me down.

AWAKENING TO PURPOSE

After a year of college, I had a bit of a wake-up call, which offered enough clarity to realize I didn't want to be in college anymore. Perhaps I didn't even want to be *me* anymore, so I did something bold and joined the military to become an Army Ranger.

My friends thought I was crazy, my family *knew* I was crazy; but to me, my future could not have been more clear. I had a list of a hundred reasons why I wanted to join the military, which ranged from patriotism to seeing the world to becoming an elite member of Special Operations. A part of most every boy wants to do that, I suppose, but that part of me didn't grow up. So I enlisted. It felt adventurous, purposeful, like I was finally joining something outside of myself—something greater.

The next chapter of life in the military would bring some of the most significant changes I ever experienced. I became an entirely different person within a span of just a few years. My word changed from *Party*, but instead of it being replaced with *Ranger*, I was completely sideswiped by a word I certainly didn't see coming.

Jesus.

Upon joining the military, and before any of the hard stuff with drill sergeants and smoke sessions rushed upon me, I experienced a heart-shattering conversion. At this time, one of the most significant people to ever influence me came into my life. Kevin Rinehart was there with me in those early days of in-processing at the 30th Adjutant General Battalion at Fort Benning. And he changed my life.

I don't have the greatest memory for people and places, but I vividly remember Kevin. In those days, we would stand all day in lines for medical exams, haircuts, dog tags, and new military uniforms. In between all that was a lot of sitting around. No one was yelling at us at this time. The challenges of basic training still lay ahead, and for the time being we felt safe. We were young, bald soldiers hanging around on bunks telling all sorts of lies and half-truths from our former lives. I was one of them, recounting wins I'd had at partying and luck in love (or better said, lust). There was so much ego and sizing up that Kevin stood out all the more.

Kevin was a Christian, a *real* one, and I could tell the difference. I'd known a ton of Christians in my life, had even claimed to be one in the past, but Kevin was different. He was encouraging, thoughtful, levelheaded, and intense.

From that time, I remember a stocky, loud-mouthed dude talking trash in the barracks. Clearly, this guy thought he was destined to be the next soldier of fortune. Kevin stepped up to a challenge this guy issued one day, then went on to smoke him in a push-up contest. After that, I loved Kevin immediately. Looking back, what was odd about him was that he never really pushed any Jesus stuff on me in spite of clearly being a committed Christian. He had no idea what was going on in my heart, didn't know I was on the cusp of a life change. This man was a living rebuke to me and a living welcome, and an invitation to something more than I could be on my own. He had something I didn't, and I couldn't place what it was.

It's hard to describe, but I felt like my heart was being broken for no good reason. I couldn't call home. For the length of about a week, I felt as though I might burst into tears at any moment. Something in me was breaking apart for good, and it needed to be. I was not the man I should be, and I knew it. There was a greater calling out there for my life, and it went beyond the military.

Looking back, this feeling is still a bit mystifying to me. I wasn't homesick, as I had moved out at age fifteen to attend boarding school and then on to college. I wasn't weak (by all accounts, I was a pretty tough dude at this point). But something was, nonetheless, missing. Everything I had done up to that point was a form of searching, grasping for some unattainable ideal just beyond reach, like the green light in *The Great Gatsby*, always evasively taunting one ambitious man's abilities.

A lot of men feel this way, I think: they know they are capable of something more, but it seems to elude them. They can't get it or even name it most of the time. Maybe this is because we cannot reach it of our own accord. We need help getting to our best selves, finding our purpose.

Maybe some searches can only be done with the soul.

On May 20, 2001, my inner anguish came to a tipping point. Though it had been building for some time, I suddenly had a profound drive to devote my life to Jesus. I wanted to laugh but cried instead. For a week, I had been on the verge of breaking; and now, I was shattering into a thousand pieces. I was being "saved," but it felt like death. It was the most terrifying moment of my life, because everything I had ever been was gone.

Who would I be now? I was about to find out.

That was the most dramatic point in my life, altering the course of who I would become. Never again would *Play*, *Cool*, *Winning*, *Party*, or any other pursuit define me. I would not settle for ego or vanity and would not look to any more false muses. Surely, I'd be distracted again; but I knew these were costumes I had worn, just like the boy playing in the woods.

For years, I had been running away from what I could be, and now it was all catching up to me. Every man finds clever ways to dodge truth and goodness until he can't. He distracts himself with games and silly little contests and ego trips. But all that was over for me. I had just donned a new identity and within a week was about to start a journey of constant pain and testing. But my heart was ready. Finally, I had found something greater than myself to live for—a true and lasting reason for living, a purpose beyond my wildest imagination.

MUSES GUIDE US

As I look back on my past, I realize I stumbled a lot in the dark and was sometimes even stumbled upon. I found a wild and free spirit in the woods of my youth, which was part of me—but not all of me. On occasion, I still yearn to get lost in the wilderness, ride motorcycles, rock climb, jump out of planes, and suck adventure from life wherever I can. That feeling never left, but it no longer defines me.

Today, on a good day, I am fully alive and intend to stay that way until I am fully dead. I found gritty strength and determination in wrestling. I could keep going long after others would quit and was supremely stubborn even in supreme pain. I found a warrior in the military, as well as virtue and passion in my faith. I found a poet when I met my wife—who became my muse—and I found gentleness as a father. But I found freedom and purpose only in Jesus. Now, with Him at the center, I am left to bring all these areas into balance. I am not *one* of these things. I am all of them, and so are you. At least, you can be.

A purpose grounds a man, helping him find his center. For my part, I pick Jesus, my eternal source of inspiration. In Him, I see a strength I do not possess. I'd love to be like Him but don't come close. Not yet. Still, He is my ideal, the example I am striving for, the purpose pointing me to something greater than I am while offering hope for what I could be.

Even if you are an atheist or a member of a different religion, it would be hard to deny the far-reaching impact of this man. To cite the celebrated historian Will Durant, whom I referenced earlier, "The outlines of the life, character, and the teaching of Christ, remain reasonably clear, and constitute the most fascinating feature of the history of Western Man." Now, keep in mind that this is a secular man who has examined the evidence and gives full recognition that there is something incomparably remarkable about the historical Jesus. That's a purpose worthy of inspiring all of us, at least in my opinion.

Jesus is the man who split time in two. Just take a look at your calendar. See what year it is? That's how many years we've seen since the beginning of the Common Era. And yet, time doesn't begin at year zero. What restarts history's clock? The birth of Jesus, of course. That's significant when you think about it. Before you relegate this to mere religious propaganda, try to appreciate the reality of that for a moment. All history, secular or religious, points to an important historical divide: BC or AD. The past puts Jesus in the center, which is a pretty big deal. Consider the alleged reflections of the famous war commander Napoleon Bonaparte:

> I know men, and I tell you that Jesus Christ is not a man. . . . Every thing in him astonishes me. His spirit overawes me, and his will confounds me. Between him and whoever else in the world there is no possible term of comparison.

If we're going to have some source of inspiration, wouldn't you want one who is more than human? I would. The point is not whether or not you believe this man was or is the son of God. That's up to you, and every man has to make that decision himself. The point is that having a deep source of inspiration beyond what you can imagine is essential to fulfilling your calling as a man. Nothing else will satisfy.

You and I are likely not so different, not that we have the same circumstances or that you went into the military or wrestled in high school. But I bet you have wandered through the woods of your own past in search of an adventure big enough to give your whole life to. I bet you have yearned for a life filled to the brim with passion and meaning, something so profound you'd be willing to die for it, if necessary. I bet you have wondered if life is a series of cosmic accidents or if you are here for a reason, called to a purpose beyond your own comfort.

I know this because every man I have ever met has hungered for these things. He has faced his own selfishness and felt it war with his conscience. He has beheld the muse and pursued her. He has heard the call of fear trying to lull him back to sleep and knows that a dreamy existence free of conflict is not enough.

Have you found a muse who inspires you to live a deeper life? Has that muse helped you find a purpose that guides your entire life? Whoever or whatever it may be, may your muse challenge you to be better today than you were yesterday, helping you find a purpose that is worth your whole life, one worthy of your commitment.

A MUSE WILL BALANCE YOU

To more analytical minds, this may all sound a bit flowery and poetic, maybe even religious. What of the firm structure of the natural sciences and of logic? I have a very analytical side that defaults to the unbending rules of reason, so I get it. My contention, though, is the dichotomy that sets faith against reason, and the arts against science, is a false one. It is not one or the other, but both-and.

Diminishing either warrior or poet leaves the scales lacking in the essentials of a balanced man. A man is at his best when he has cultivated two crucial elements of himself: the defender and lover. These elements are not at odds but flow into each other. Real love protects, and protectors love that which they protect. A muse helps us find this balance, giving us something to fight for and someone to love. When these elements are not in harmony, a man will wander into vain and destructive places. The balance he should live by will be skewed and broken. A muse anchors him in his convictions, calls him deeper into his purpose. And to an extent, all relationships can do this.

Our relationships in life are one of the only things that make life worth the struggle. Whether it be as a captain at war or a captain of industry, the battles we fight are not the reason we are here. The wars we wage are a means to an end, and that end is relationship. Nothing matters more than that. No one on their deathbed asks for bank statements, trophies, or mementos. They ask for family and friends. They say prayers to God. They peer into the void and ask, "Did I make my life count for something that will endure?"

Jesus once said, "For what will it profit a man if he gains the whole world, and loses his own soul?" Nothing. It's a fantastic reality check, really. It's not money or success, not power or stuff that ultimately satisfies you. Living for a higher purpose and investing in people is all you can hope to fulfill you. That's it. That's where we find a truly meaningful life.

True success comes in sacrificing for others and nurturing healthy relationships; a life lived well is one in total service to others. This sort of sacrifice is so counter to our selfish natures that we often groan under doing what we know we should. How much easier is it to spend money on what we want rather than on charitable causes and helping the less fortunate? It's so much more satisfying—today, at least—to scroll social media, play video games, obsess over sports, and binge-watch TV shows, than to give our time and attention to people.

I'm not grandstanding or shaming anyone, mind you, because I keenly feel the weight of my own inadequacy in this area. I'm not yet living up to my own ideal, as I have selfishly squandered too much of my life in the pursuit of my own vain comfort. So I know from experience how uninspiring that can be, how easily I can give up the chase when things get hard. My muse keeps me focused on what my life ought to be about, reminding me lovingly when I am falling short.

COMMITMENT CREATES CHARACTER

How do we find our muse, then? Well, let me tell you that it is not enough to find yourself a pretty girl, pursue her, and marry her. Even writing her some poetry and performing some big act of courage right in front of her is not sufficient. This is what Rebekah taught me almost day one of our relationship: love demands our all.

What love needs to grow, more than incredibly romantic gestures or grand displays of courage, is commitment. Plain and simple. Keep pursuing your muse, that woman who captured your heart in a single moment and refused to let go. You must never stop the chase, even when it looks like you've gotten what you sought. Commit to a lifetime pursuit of her, and she will always take you deeper than you could go on your own.

Far too often, we lose sight of this, mistaking our next mission for a deeper purpose, forsaking everyone and everything we were fighting for. We discard the kids and wife for something exciting and shiny, thinking they'll understand "someday." When we do this, we split our attention and love in multiple directions, and everything suffers. Commitment is key to sustained purpose and meaning in our lives.

Similarly, we seem to think that a hot, budding romance in the beginning of a relationship is enough to sustain us into "happily ever after." It's not. After the honeymoon phase has passed—and it will—your relationship is yours to grow or kill. And honestly, growing it can be thankless, frustrating, humbling, and long-suffering work.

I don't promise any of this will be easy. In fact, I promise it will be hard, but it will be worth it. Love your muse, and she will take you further than you could have ever gone on your own. You will find deep joy and love together, regardless of outward achievements or lack thereof. Even if you find yourself miserable at present, do the work, commit to the process, and see what unexpected blessings result. But they will come only if and when you commit.

Commitment to your muse is not merely an intellectual exercise. It's not even one of pure will. It requires your heart, as well.

Hundreds of times over the years, I've seen a familiar pattern affecting soldiers. Men fall in love, get married, then go through an ugly divorce after neglecting their brides for years. What, exactly, happened? Absence definitely takes a toll on these relationships. When soldiers go off to war, a rift can grow between them and their wives, sure, but that's not typically why these relationships die. In contrast, I've seen lifelong military men maintain successful marriages for decades. What happens to the majority of warriors whose relationships fail is that they never learn to embrace their own inner poet. They major in some pieces of masculinity but don't delve into other areas that are essential to keeping relationships alive.

Far too often, when the warrior comes home, he fails to be sweet, soft, and vulnerable to the woman he loves. Yes, she wants a man who can protect her, one who is dangerous in all the right ways. But in all the in-between times, when you are not defending the home or providing for the family, she's got to learn to live with a brute. And if you remain a big, dumb brute at all times, you aren't easy to live with. She needs compliments far more often than she needs to see you warding off ninjas lurking behind the shed.

When you treat your wife the way you treat the guys, you lose her. Contrary to the current messaging of our backward culture, a woman is different from a man. She needs you to be the warrior on the battlefield of life and a poet in the home. Learning to strike this balance is difficult but, again, worth it.

At some point in life, dear warrior, you will fall in love, as I did that fateful day. It is an incredible and awful feeling. There's nothing like it. It will overpower you and leave you feeling vulnerable at the same time, scared in ways that might even seem foreign to you. Falling in love is a powerful sensation, to be sure, one that causes men to do incredible things. It's a good start to a beautiful relationship, but it is not enough to sustain a lifelong commitment. We must, in fact, learn *to* love. This is not natural for men in the sense that they know how to give a woman what she needs in each and every moment. Love is a verb, an endless pursuit, one that just keeps giving. Otherwise, we become another unfortunate statistic.

This stuff isn't easy, which is why we decide ahead of time we are in it for the long haul. As Mark Twain wrote, "Love seems the swiftest, but it is the slowest of all growths. No man or woman really knows what perfect love is until they have been married a quarter of a century." The type of resolve is romantic even if it doesn't feel that way at times. It's not necessarily popular, but it is good. From a deep commitment comes great love, clarity, and purpose.

MEN AND MARRIAGE

One of the best callings in life that a man can answer is the call to committed relationship. Namely, marriage. But what does that even mean these days?

I am constantly irritated by the presentation of love stories by

Hollywood on the big screen. Invariably, it's almost always about the initial falling in love, not slugging it out with gritty commitment in year seven when you are disagreeing and life has you on the ropes. Quite the contrary, when someone is unhappy in an on-screen marriage, the story can justify affairs and divorces. It is as if the greatest ideal they can muster is personal happiness that comes from how a new romance makes a person *feel*. The vows our movie characters take are more like, "I will love you forever as long as you keep making me *feel* happy."

I have a much different view of marriage that is far removed from what our current culture preaches. I'm anchored to what the ancient biblical covenant prescribes. A covenant is much more than a contract; it's a deep commitment that binds two souls together. Marriage is a spiritual agreement to tough out the hard times and celebrate the good ones. In old wedding ceremonies, the vows went something like this: "I promise to love you for better or *worse*, for richer, for poorer, in sickness and in health." Think about that for a moment. It means I'll love you even if you get fat, poor, sick, and make me miserable. I'll love you forever because that is what I'm committing to. It's a one-sided promise that does not demand action on the other person's part.

Fortunately, the spouse typically makes the same one-sided promise, but the point is it's not a contract. There is no quid-pro-quo exchange. Even if the other person doesn't make you happy, you still keep your promise—in action, even if not in feeling. It's a gritty, long-suffering, stubborn kind of love. That's what you are signing up for.

Now, of course, there are allowances for abuse and infidelity, and sometimes things don't work out. You can't make another person want to stay committed to you, no matter how hard you try; some marriages just end. There's no shame in that, per se, and you have my empathy. But my point here is that a covenant is a deeper calling than "this feels good for right now," and when both people take it seriously, it offers a beautiful opportunity to grow and become a better person.

Loving when you don't feel like it is tough work, but it forges you into a more loving person. The point of the marriage covenant isn't to make you happy, necessarily, but to make you holy. Holiness often brings about happiness but better still, joy. Joy is an inner peace and affirmation of value that stays even when you are feeling the turmoil of unhappiness through hard times. If we become holy, we can have joy even when we feel like we're being sawed in two and our lives are falling apart. Sometimes, it may feel like your spouse is the one doing the sawing! No matter your circumstance, you can still have everlasting joy, which is why our love must be sustained by commitment, and that commitment should be rooted in deep purpose. Joy is long-lasting and long-suffering. Purpose and commitment allow us to love at times when the happiness fades, but the joy does not.

Some people become obsessed with that initial feeling of falling in love. It's understandable. After all, this experience can be a whirlwind of passion, but it is such a dangerous trap. Often, we are falling in love with the feeling of love versus truly loving the person in front of us. Don't believe me? Consider the many characters in Shakespearean plays who could so quickly fall in and out of love with one another. These romances usually found themselves within Shakespeare's comedies because the results were always disastrous messes that were good for a few laughs.

The underlying truth here is that those who can fall so quickly in love can fall very quickly out of love. Love, when a feeling without any grounding in commitment, can come and go like the wind. That kind of "love" is less about knowing another person and bravely committing to them for the long haul and is more indicative of a person who has a deep need inside of them that needs to be filled. They are an incomplete person looking for someone to make them whole. And it never works.

If you have that big of a hole, you desperately need someone to fill it, and what you're infatuated with is a person that makes you feel a certain way. This is a condition many poets know well; the work here is to balance your ease of falling in love with some strength, commitment, and a sober assessment of the person you are in a relationship with. There can be no room made for wishful thinking amplified by temporary passionate feelings. Love is more than a fleeting feeling; it is a deep and lasting commitment. And in that deep connection to another person, which at times can look like a trap to the uninitiated, there is, ironically, deep freedom and belonging.

THE WARRIOR AND POET IN LOVE

My wife calls me the "Needless Man." She gets hungry whenever her blood sugar crashes, which means she needs to eat every few hours or so. I, on the other hand, can go days without eating and sometimes do. I can sleep less and push myself physically further than she can. I can lift heavier stuff, and my body can take more damage. I'm stronger physically, but it's a joke to say I'm needless, because she knows full well how much I need and rely on her.

What I appreciate about Rebekah is that she recognizes our differences and that we both have qualities that complement each other. That's why a husband and wife make such a good team. My wife's emotional wherewithal keeps our relationship healthy, because she notices first if anything is "off." She's able to multitask and nurture and educate our kids in a way that is foreign and fantastic to me. She makes my hard work worth it, giving vitality and passion to our life. As a crown jewel to her many strengths, she was also given beauty to allure me.

A woman is given beauty to attract, and a man is given strength to pursue. What a perfect design! Such a contrast keeps us rolling through the years of our relationship as we get wrinkled by the trials of life. She never stops drawing me in, and I never stop chasing her. Which works great, so long as we both do our part: she wants my strength, and I want her beauty.

But even that is not enough to make a relationship go the distance. To love well, men have to balance both sides of themselves:

the warrior and the poet. While it's true that a woman is attracted to the masculinity of a fighter, there's nothing to connect with if he has no inner poet. The poet is the one who offers
depth of emotion and thinking. Yes, it's important to be strong,
but it's also good to recognize your own areas of need and sensitivity. We have to bring our whole selves to our muses and let
them teach us what we are lacking.

This is why commitment in a relationship is so important. It
takes time for us to figure out which parts of ourselves are not
being called forth, and if we're hopping around from one partner to the next, we'll never grow into the men we could be. The
poet may be able to teach the warrior to love better, but the
warrior can help the poet appreciate the long-standing grit of
doing difficult things even when he doesn't want to do them. If
only the warrior could take his physical discipline and pass it to
the poet for use in the hard times of a relationship. And, for that
matter, if only the warrior himself could realize his grit is meant
for more than just physical training. Again, balance is what we
want in order to do relationship well.

Many young men I know worry about finding "the right
girl," but that, in my opinion, is not the biggest problem they
face. If you're a decent guy and you go out to meet people, you'll
likely have little problem finding a woman to love. The issue
isn't, is *she* out there for you; but rather, are *you* ready for her?

I worry when the poet seeking beauty finds the beautiful
woman and blows it, because it can create an unfortunately
common pattern: *Young Man finds Muse and chases her. Before*

long, that becomes a drag, so Young Man finds New Beauty and follows her to her bedroom. Young Man repeats this process until his entire life becomes unhinged. This may feel exciting at first, but ultimately it won't fulfill anyone. To be a great lover, you need the open heart of the poet as well as the grit of the soldier. Both make a relationship work.

Granted, even this balance doesn't safeguard us from conflict. Rather, the model of the Warrior Poet gives us a road map for how to handle the inevitable challenges that come with any relationship. When I get angry at my spouse, even after fifteen years of marriage in what I'd consider a mostly fairy-tale romance, I can still be a jerk. You've probably done the same to your loved ones. Something annoying happens, your temper starts to rise, and you say, "I'm not talking about this anymore."

Then the other person retorts, "Well, why don't you think about how you can actually help around here for a change?"

Then you see red and explode: *"What!?* Me! Not help around here? For your information . . . *I'm killing myself!"* Then you rage until you calm down a bit and muster the strength to apologize for being an idiot—again. It's a cycle most men know too well. All this is sadly normal and sometimes seemingly unavoidable. This is why we need a purpose to ground us and guide us, something deeper than even romantic love. Again, a relationship helps us see our own shortcomings and where we must grow.

For my part, I find faith to be a necessary component to any lasting relationship, mostly because I keep screwing it up with my wife, even after all this time. Try to be morally perfect some time, and you'll realize how unlike Jesus the whole world is. For this reason, the toughest man who ever walked the earth, a man who died believing He was sacrificing Himself for the entire world, wins my vote for the Greatest Warrior Poet the world has ever seen. He is more than a muse worthy of my attention and pursuit; He is the reason for my being, and I would gladly give my life for Him.

Muses, you see, must lead us into a life larger than we could imagine for ourselves, one that requires sacrifice and relationship— and those just might be the same thing.

SHE IS NO SWAN

Some mistook her for a swan.
An awkward youth that,
Almost overnight,
Shed drab feathers
And burst upon sleepy waters
In an unexpectant dazzle of white.
But I know she is no swan.
Now elegance IS hers.
Beauty, no question.
But I, who know her best,
Can tell you surely,

She is a dragon.
She hid herself from a graying world
Where none could seek her out.
There is beauty in her movement.
There is hot passion in her chest.
And she—a powerful spirit slumbering,
held treasure in her coils.
It was I who ventured for her.
I was carried, spellbound after
As she, my great quest, beckoned.
But at last in finding a fragile swan,
In waking transformed into a fearful form.
And she smiled and met my gaze
As sleep fell from her eyes.
We faced each other, transfixed.
I, a conqueror.
Her, the never conquered.
"Am I worthy?" I asked myself
As my hands trembled
And my legs went weak.
But I set my eyes and dared to try.
Sensing this, the dragon inched closer,
And I saw past dread to a fearful delight.
She smiled back.
Dumbstruck, I dropped my shield.
My armor fell beside it.
My sword I tossed behind me.

And, moving closer still, she paused,
To draw my last and first breath.
I raised my hands high.
As her fire scorched my bones . . .

that I might burn for her, Forever.

—JOHN LOVELL

PRACTICUM

What inspires you?

Who are your muses?

Take some time and think about these sources of inspiration. If you're married, remember how you used to pursue your woman when you were dating. Have you stopped chasing her as much, your relationship growing stale?

Do that stuff again. You know what I'm talking about: when you couldn't wait to take her out again. Dates, dancing, and lots of laughing.

Neglect can make a muse grow distant, but those fires can be relit with some effort and intentionality.

Are you wanting to grow in your faith or deepen in your purpose? "Draw near to God, and He will draw near to you" (James 4:8). Wherever you find your muse, whether in the sky, in the forest, in a book, or even in bed, keep your muses well-adored and they will move your very soul.

7

Learn to Dance

Life's a dance you learn as you go. Sometimes you lead, sometimes you follow.

—JOHN MICHAEL MONTGOMERY

When I was twenty years old, I went with my girlfriend at the time to an event that had swing dancing. I had never done this before and was a little nervous. Fortunately, there was a dance instructor there who walked us newbies through the steps. This hypermotivated and overly charismatic middle-aged man got up and demanded full-crowd participation, proceeding to show us the "one, two, rock-step" of swing dancing. He never stopped smiling from ear to ear as he told us how *easy* it was to just, "ONE, TWO, ROCK-STEP!"

Meanwhile, I was finding the rock step difficult and couldn't catch on. As our happy, yet very irritating instructor centered on me, he didn't provide the secret instruction I was seeking. Instead, he showed me that *he* could one, two, rock-step and that, of course, it was *easy*—lest I forget that important point amid my obvious failure. It was at this moment that I knew I wanted to punch this man in the nose. I wondered how he'd respond with me standing over him as he bled out, saying, "See? Getting punched is *easy*!" Fortunately for him (and me), the evening passed without incident. I remained a rock-step failure, and he remained unpunched.

Fast-forward several years, and I was now in the military: a combat veteran, surrounded by men all the time in what might be one of the most testosterone-laden environments ever. I missed being around girls and wanted a reprieve from Rangering. For whatever reason, I remembered Mr. One, Two, Rock-Step and decided to take up swing dancing again. Slowly, painfully, and secretly, I went dancing on weekends. At those gatherings, I wasn't an elite killer or combat veteran, but just John, the amazingly average swing dancer. It was nice.

Over time, I learned the rock step and a handful of other moves, and as my skill increased, it became more fun. Somewhere along the way, I got pretty good and reluctantly grew in my confidence as a dancing killer. Later, it was a joy to teach my wife to swing dance, and we've been dancing through our fifteen years of marriage ever since. Lord willing, we will dance through the next fifty together.

Swing dancing didn't just teach me to woo a woman (but

let's not overlook that very important part). It also taught me to interact with life in a more fluid way. When you're out on the dance floor, you don't get to choose what song comes next. You don't get to control whom you might bump into when everyone starts rock-stepping around one another. Dancing is the art of learning to maneuver around things; it's the act of balancing as best you can in an unsteady and unpredictable environment.

Swing dancing was a great stress reliever for me, but it also reinforced the same lessons I was learning in Ranger Battalion, chiefly that you can't control everything that comes your way. You can, however, control how you react. So, whether it was dancing or fighting, I was learning to let go and listen to the "music" of life, making the most of every situation.

If you want to be a Warrior Poet, a verifiable lion and lamb, you've got to learn to dance, at least figuratively; but come on, let's take it literally, too. It's a good idea, and girls go for it—big time.

THE UNBALANCED MAN

Imagine a man who works very hard at his job and comes home exhausted. His wife, who also works hard, has a running list of daily honey-do items that needs his attention. He keeps putting these things off until he can find a little more time and energy. The grass needs to be cut, the power bill is overdue, the dog needs to go to the vet, and a tire on one of the cars is leaking.

When this man comes through the door from a long day of

work, he wants nothing more than to fall into his favorite chair for some much-needed peace and quiet. But there's a pile of his laundry there that needs to be folded and put away. In the other room, he hears the kids fighting; and in the next moment, one is crying hysterically. His wife calls from another room, reminding him that they are going to dinner tonight with the neighbors. Rest will have to remain out of reach for a while longer. How long? Who knows. This is life for most men.

The average man moves from one scene in life to the next, constantly burdened by what must be done. He is aware of the obligations that need to be filled, the tasks that haven't been completed, the people who require his attention. Almost every day brings with it a whole new set of issues that threaten to overwhelm him. This man always has something to do, someone to please, some problem to occupy his mind. There's always more work than time available, more needs from his family than he can afford, and more causes that require his energy.

For a while, a man can handle these demands, if he's strong and disciplined. But eventually the pressure becomes unbearable. After enough time, the man will either snap or he will simply shut down, allowing burnout to run its course. He will become a shell of a man, a ghost in his own life, moving from one moment to the next like a robot. If he's lucky, he will muster just enough energy to get above the line, then dive immediately back into responsibilities, resetting the vicious cycle.

You can imagine, similarly, a wife who's juggling a career and trying to be the glue that holds the family together. She shoulders the lion's share of childcare and does her best to keep a tidy home and put food on the table. Even harder, imagine a single mother doing the same. Life's difficult with all the things that require a person's heart, strength, and mind; but it's even harder when you have to do it on your own! Neither of these scenarios, for the man or woman, can be sustained for long. We need balance, and we all struggle to create it.

Balance is the ticket to long-term success, in my experience. If you are a successful businessman but an absentee father, that's not success. If you're crushing your quarterly goals but a stranger to your wife, you have not won at life. Not yet. Why is this so difficult for most men? Because balance is not natural to us. It must be learned, practiced.

In the work that I do, it's common to find men who are physically strong but spiritually weak. They plow through life with pure tenacity and grit, knocking down any obstacle in their way. This works—for a while. But if you never develop long-term internal fortitude, something in life will break you, no matter how much you can deadlift. Personally, I don't want to crush it at the gym and not be growing mentally. If I can kill something from five hundred meters away but don't have the courage to face an upset wife, that is not what it means to be a strong man. What's the point of being strong if your strength can't help you weather emotional and physical storms?

Of course, the opposite is true, too. Physical strength is extremely valuable for health, energy, and work. It's no good for a man to cultivate mental and emotional strength but not discipline his body. Still, many of the trials we face in life will be tests of our internal strength. We no longer live at a time when we go out on the savanna, hunting with spears every day; nonetheless, we still struggle to survive, albeit in a world of ones and zeros instead of lions and tigers. Not much has changed, then. We just wear suits instead of loincloths. (If you are reading this while wearing only a loincloth, I apologize for marginalizing you. Also, you are likely weirding everyone out, so maybe rethink your life.)

What we need is balance, and this is created by a different kind of strength than we are accustomed to. Just like I had to learn the frustrating process of training my feet to do the one, two, rock-step, I have had to harness both my physical and mental strength to dance through life. It's not easy, nor is it always pretty; but this is how you eventually learn to navigate life without breaking anything or anyone (or at least minimizing the damage).

EMBRACE THE CHAOS

How do we do this? How do we find ways to better respond to all the responsibilities and obligations that make us want to check out? To begin, we have to stop running away. In the same way boys (and even men) are afraid to go out on the dance floor because they haven't learned the moves, we must face our greatest trials that reveal our weaknesses and insecurities. This can be frightening at first, but it's worth it.

These days, men seem to be seeking an escape from responsibility at all costs. It's an epidemic. I don't condone absconding from obligations, but I understand the desire to do so. I know why grown men get lost in hours of gaming at night and why they find convenient excuses to not go home after work. It's hard to deal with the endless stream of responsibilities and people who never stop needing things from you. Life is full of burdens and worries that are often too overwhelming to face head-on, and that's the kind of stress that can crush a man. As the great C. S. Lewis once remarked, "One is given strength to bear what happens to one, but not the one hundred and one different things that *might* happen."

Here's the good news though: those pressures that feel absolutely debilitating at times can be the same ones that bring tremendous joy, when rightly considered. You don't need to run from your life; you just need to balance it. Imagine trying to carry a mattress. It's not heavy; it's just bulky and awkward and therefore cumbersome. The same is true with life. Balancing our priorities can be tough when we don't know how to wield them. Or, as someone once said, "It's not the load that breaks you down, it's the way you carry it."

This is what I mean when I say we've got to learn to dance: with women, life, and daily responsibilities. We can't force life to happen the way we want, but we can move with it. We can't make all our responsibilities go away, but we can carry them better.

If we don't understand how to keep the demands on our time

in balance, the result will be disaster. We see this all around us: men leaving their families for an easier life, marriages ending in heartbreak, the tragic stereotype of some dude sitting on a barstool after work, drowning his exhaustion in alcohol. All these are signposts to us, reminders that before we can do better we must become better. We cannot ask life to be less than it is; we cannot change the mattress's shape. We can, however, do everything possible to strategize and strengthen ourselves to carry it.

Dancing is the process of balancing with another, moving through a space filled with all kinds of unexpected conflicts and challenges. This requires letting go of what we cannot control and embracing what we can. Dancing with life means balancing all the demands on your time and energy and embracing them.

The first sign I see in a man whose existence is already imploding is expectations. He wants things to be some other way than how they actually are. He wants more money and stuff, but less responsibility and headaches, and that's not how life works. Expectations can steal your joy and destroy your self-worth. They can deprive you of the wonder of the moment and the battle you are called to fight. We must recognize when things don't go our way, using these disappointments as prompts to keep moving with the music.

As overwhelming as it may seem, the first step is to take the first step. Learning to swing dance was beyond frustrating for me. I almost quit more than once but kept going back because I saw something in the art form that attracted me: *balance*. I knew that it was going to be a struggle to learn but that such a skill would be useful for years to come. The same is true with how we balance our lives. It will take time, practice, and stumbling; but the result is worth the struggle.

You can't make every stressor go away today, but you can start dancing with the chaos. Move the laundry off the chair and close your eyes for five minutes of peace. As you hop up with a little renewed energy, engage the kids in a quick wrestle to distill their conflict, then ask your wife what's needed for the neighbors. After that, you may find a little more energy comes, so before bed tonight you decide to dive into the book you've been putting off and set your alarm a little earlier for a workout tomorrow. You manage the frazzled circumstances with more preparation, not necessarily more rest. Doing nothing doesn't help, but chopping it all up into smaller pieces that you can attack one at a time does. Action, however small, is key.

GET YOUR AMBITION BACK

To dance well with life, we have to get some of our gusto back. We need to push ourselves harder than we think we can go. It may sound counterintuitive, but this is necessary. I know you're tired, worn out, and frustrated. The good news is that you were built for this and may not even know it.

Most men don't come close to what their real limits are. They can carry more burdens than they know. If you think you can run two miles, I guarantee I could get you to run five, if you let me push you. You can go harder than you think, and you can do just about anything longer than you believe you can.

Most men have more to give and they settle for too little. If you are the type of guy who is apathetic, unmotivated, and living anything resembling a sedentary lifestyle, you don't need to know your limits so you can stop exceeding them. You need to put your nose down and work harder. This kind of man is tired not because he's doing too much but because he's doing too little.

If you are casually walking through the marathon of life with a burrito in hand, stopping for breaks along the way, you need to wake up. It's not time to take a nap; it's time to charge even harder. You're bored, not exhausted; apathetic, not overwhelmed. You've got to get your ambition back. Otherwise, the slightest problem or mishap is going to derail you. Part of learning to dance is building up the muscles to take those basic steps.

To begin, let's look for ambition-robbing activities you're engaging in. Your soul thirsts for true adventure and victory, not distraction and leisure. You should find those in your work, in how you serve your community and world, and in walking side by side with your loved ones. When you power up a gaming system, however, that allows you to enter a new world and save the galaxy from intergalactic destruction without leaving your couch, your soul is fed a cheap substitute for the real conquest.

Similarly, you are made for true connection and depth. But when pornography replaces the need for real intimacy your wife should be satisfying, your relationship begins to die among your misplaced and twisted passions. You are feeding your soul lies instead of seeking out the truth in the real world. When you vicariously live through the heroes on your screens and get your taste of victory from a favorite sports team, your ambition is being robbed.

These time-wasting and passion-sucking activities can leave you an unmotivated shell of a man who has spent his vitality on cheap counterfeits. You've been robbed of your greatest resource, and it's time to steal it back. Replace your bad habits with good ones. Put down the unhealthy snacks and pick up some weights. Go pursue your wife even if she's mad at you (especially then). Stop collecting digital accolades in cyberspace and find some real value. Parasites are taking your passions and leaving you empty. We have to cut them out before the cancer infects the whole body.

Start now, before it's too late, and marvel at how much more energy you have once you get moving.

RESPECT YOUR LIMITS

Perhaps, a lack of motivation is not your problem. Maybe, like me, you don't know your own limits and often push yourself *too* hard. This is equally dangerous. Again, our ideal here is balance, not perfection. The goal is to move through the world well, responding calmly to all kinds of chaos as it comes. As we build back up our ambition, reclaiming what we've likely given away to all kinds of unworthy forces, we need to know and respect our limits.

You cannot live up to everyone's expectations and meet everyone's needs. You just can't. If you gave work everything it would like to demand of you, it would keep demanding more until it had taken every shred of your attention from all other areas of life. Consider that your boss will always want a little more tomorrow based on what you can deliver today. That's just the nature of work. But you can easily dig yourself an early grave if you don't know your limits. Be careful here; many men give too much to work and deprive the rest of their lives as a result.

Your family will also always want more, too. More of your time, more of your attention, more of your love. They may even want more stuff: a bigger house, a new bike, the latest gaming system, and so on. Kids have no concept of "enough" or of consequences. Like all of us, they have to understand there is a cost to everything, and some things take time and extra hard work to get. Some of us never learn this lesson and end up striving for "more" without ever appreciating what we have. It may come as a surprise that I'm advocating limits on what you're able to give to the people you love, but it can be a loving act to say no. Our family and friends don't always know what they're asking of us—they know only what they want—and it's our job to help them understand.

You will never be able to give everything to everyone who wants something from you. This includes your woman, your children, your boss, your parents, your friends, everyone. You are human, and humans can do only so much at once. If you're giving to others, there will always be more needs to meet and more hands out waiting to be filled. Maybe you're stuck trying to please a father who was never satisfied, not because you're not good enough but because his expectations were unrealistic. That's not your fault, but it becomes your responsibility if you don't know what you are capable of.

Similarly, you won't always be able to give yourself everything you want. "Enough" is never a constant. Have you noticed that you always want a little more money, a little more prestige, a little more respect? It may be the nature of ambition, which is good to have, but you've got to keep it in check.

I'm not anti-ambition, clearly. It's good to want things and be willing to work hard for them. After all, you don't want to be the checked-out drifter: content with mediocrity, scared of commitment, unwilling to face conflict. That is not a successful man; that is a directionless man. Ambition can be healthy, but it can also easily devolve into something unhealthy, making you greedy, selfish, and narrow-minded. You've got to say no even to yourself, and this is called self-discipline. You have only so much to give, and if you try to exceed what's possible, you won't be able to support the people you love for long.

None of this is an invitation to be lazy or to stop serving. You should be carrying a huge burden as a man. It's why, after all, we were given strength. You're built for providing and defending, so don't shirk your responsibilities and don't neglect your strength. Notice when you are out of balance and when the load might need some lightening. You have your limits and if you find yourself in a season of driving and pushing hard, it may be that you are exceeding what you are capable of right now. Again, an important lesson in dancing is knowing how to move around the room. There are, in fact, legitimate limitations we all have to be aware of. The result of ignoring these realities is not pretty.

Limits are given to us by life. You actually can lift only a certain amount of weight right now. You have only so many hours in a day and so much energy to give. These are real limits that you can try to push, but they will eventually push back. We have to listen to them when they do and learn what they are trying to teach us. That said, there is another kind of limit that is not given to us, but one we can create. And this is called a boundary.

SET BOUNDARIES

Once you know where your limits are, you can decide how much is enough to give in each area of life. These are your boundaries, what you're willing to commit to in terms of energy and time. Everyone and everything in your life can demand more than you can give, so with incredible discipline, protect what you can offer. Asserting boundaries and saying no to people we care about and don't want to disappoint is not normal, but it is necessary. A man who knows what his lane is and how to stay in it is a man who can live a full life.

My high school wrestling coach demanded 110 percent from me. Ignoring the mathematical impossibility of this, this was simply good old-fashioned coaching. All coaches want you to give more than you think you can give, and that teaches us a lesson about what we can actually accomplish, especially when we're younger. But practically speaking, this kind of intensity is hard to sustain.

To give 110 percent to wrestling, I had my diet perfectly tuned for the sport. I didn't share the same meals my family ate but instead had a more disciplined approach. I woke up before sunrise and went to the gym for a run before school. In school, I daydreamed about wrestling when I should have been paying attention in class. I even sketched out moves and drills I wanted to work on during practice.

In the interest of cutting weight to be in a lower weight class, on weigh-in days I avoided eating anything, including lunch, and timed my water fountain visits to not take on too much water weight. I crushed myself in practice and stayed when it was over to continue working after the others had stopped. Then I went to the gym again for more punishment and ended it all with some time in the sauna.

When I got home, I skipped dinner and collapsed early from exhaustion. If a wrestling match weigh-in was in a couple of days, I slept in a trash bag with holes in it to make a "sweatshirt" to get rid of excess weight at night. Another trick was turning the air conditioner up and sleeping without covers so that I shivered all night, cutting even more weight.

Some of this sounds insane, I'm sure, but it was my life for a couple years in high school. All this came to a head, however, when I was cutting fifteen to seventeen pounds each week to make weight for the next wrestling match. I barely ate anything at all in the last two or three days leading up to the match so I could still make weight. I knew that I had been giving too much to the sport when my parents started to believe I was going to kill myself.

One night at fifteen years old, I came out of the bathroom and was greeted by my mother and father sitting on my bed. I thought that was weird, because my father never came upstairs. I remember thinking something must be up, because I hadn't seen him in my room in years! My parents were there to have an intervention. Apparently, I *had* been giving wrestling 110 percent, and that was too much. They'd heard rumors of wrestlers dying earlier that year from doing similar things that I'd been doing. They were legitimately concerned for my life and should have been. I was one of the few people who didn't take this coaching merely as a motivational aphorism. I was testing my limits and was way out of balance.

You can't give more than 100 percent to every area of your life; as you maximize one area of life, you do it at the expense of another. Something has to suffer for something else to thrive. So, how, then, do you prepare for this? You set boundaries. You decide what is worth your all and what is not. Boundaries are the lines we draw beforehand to protect our energy and priorities.

Your boundaries don't have to work for other people, but they better work for you. The trick is to set them and be content with yourself even when others kick and scream about wanting more from you. If you're someone who has typically cared a lot about what others think, this can be difficult. At some point, though, you're going to let someone down. Just make sure it's the right person and for the right reasons.

PACE YOURSELF

Different seasons call for different boundaries. When I was getting close to graduating college, I shifted my focus from trying to make straight As to making all Bs. Why would I do such a thing, willingly letting go of what I understood excellence to be?

At the time, I was working forty to fifty hours a week, had a family who lived far away, and was engaged in different types of campus ministry and other activities—all while still being a full-time student. I didn't have a master's degree to prepare for, wasn't going to take the bar or MCATs or anything like that, so there was no practical reason to get that A other than my ego demanded it.

Coming to my senses, I downshifted one priority so that I could balance everything else more equitably, because those other things were just as important, if not more important, than good grades. I gave myself permission to not be perfect, which brought a lot of relief and some much-needed balance back to my life. The pace I was going at just wasn't sustainable for that particular season.

Life is a marathon, not a sprint. If you go all-out every moment, you may impress others for a while, but soon you'll run out of gas. You have to run in a way that enables you to finish the race. I remember seeing this in the military doing two-mile runs. I was never one of the big guys in Ranger Battalion, but in the words of Forrest Gump, "I could run like the wind blows." My *worst* two-mile time was somewhere around twelve minutes and thirty seconds while my best was in the low to mid-elevens. I had to put in the work to earn these low times, but I also discovered the trick to getting these times was to *pace* myself.

As a general rule, I found my second mile should always be faster than my first mile, and if I left myself enough gas during the first mile for the second, I could speed up. When the run would start, I would immediately fall into my own pace but was irritated to see a mob of soldiers pass me. Often, I would end up near the back of the pack for the first thirty seconds, which was embarrassing. One by one, however, I'd catch up to my buddies and pass them, because they hadn't paced themselves. At the end, I'd be in the top few finishers. Life is like that. You may see some people cruising on by at an unsustainable pace, but that can't last long. That's not to say there aren't times to go all-out, but most of the things that matter—work, relationships, faith—are long-term commitments that require us to pace ourselves.

You cannot give all of your energy all the time to everything. You're not a machine. You've got to rest well, eat well, and work at a reasonable and sustainable pace. You also have to know yourself, including what you and you alone can give: how hard you can work at a given time, how much energy you can invest in family and friends, and what kind of effort you can dedicate to things like fitness, training, and everything else. We all have limits, and the wise man knows what his are.

Setting boundaries is harder work than we'd sometimes like to admit. You have to be content with your output, even when others say it isn't enough. One of the greatest fears a man has is not measuring up, that what he has to offer the world is simply not enough. Women, too, struggle with this but often when it comes to their appearance and how they are accepted. Men's struggle with feeling insufficient tends to come down to their strength and performance. This nagging feeling of "not enough" can lead us into all kinds of dangerous situations, if we're not careful.

When you don't know who you are and what you can do and haven't decided that *that* is enough, you become a slave to the opinions of others. You allow other people's expectations to define what you're capable of. And this reactionary, people-pleasing way of life can be downright miserable.

I know of no other way to live a long and healthy life than to make sure that you know your limits, set healthy boundaries, and decide to be content with how the chips fall. If you're living only to please those making their demands on you, you're going to end up feeling exhausted, frustrated, and defeated. If you're reading this book (and you are), then you likely care about being better today than you were yesterday. You *want* to grow. That's good! Keep going. But don't just work harder to get there. Work smarter, accept grace when you fall short, and learn to rest. Remember that you've got to get up and do it all again tomorrow. Your success hinges on the priorities you set and how well you balance your time attacking those priorities.

Don't forget to pace yourself.

WARRIOR MEETS WOMAN

Learning to dance is about becoming more flexible with life, and this, of course, includes the maddening mystery of human relationships. It's not enough to find a muse you love and adore. Once you chase her down and win the hunt, you have to not only keep her but find new and interesting ways to keep the dance alive. Becoming a little less rigid and a little more sensitive to the needs of women can help.

Personally, I was a little low on the sensitivity spectrum. I knew how to hunt terrorists, jump out of planes, rock climb cliffs, and break people's bones with jiu-jitsu, but I hadn't figured out how to talk to girls. My high school sweetheart and I stayed together through the years as I leaped from one hypermasculine activity to the next, while she was enjoying things like sorority life and working as an interior designer. Our worlds became increasingly more different, and I remember struggling to say the right "boyfriend things." Somehow, I was getting worse at it the more I tried.

I remember one night when I was talking to her on the phone, and I somehow intuited she was upset (she was crying and saying things like, "I'm upset"—I'm sharp like that). *Good*, I thought. My training had prepared me for this very moment. It was time to initiate the sensitivity protocol. I had heard that it didn't matter so much what you said to girls as how you said it. So when my girlfriend told me of the difficulties she was experiencing, I summoned the sweetest voice you will ever hear from a Ranger and encouraged her.

"Well, you know, baby," I said, "you've just gotta . . . suck it up."

The phone went silent, then a voice that usually sounded like a little bird took on the tone of, well, a dragon.

"Suck it up!?" she growled. "SUCK IT UP!?!?"

Uh oh. Somehow, this intel I had received was not only insufficient but absolutely incorrect. Clearly, it *does* matter what you say as well as how you say it. And news flash: she didn't speak Army. It may not surprise you that we didn't stay together. Looking back now, it's a funny story because I realize how hopelessly oblivious I was in terms of relating to women. I had, somehow, after spending too much time on the ragged edge, forgotten how to be sensitive.

You've heard me so far in this book rail against the "sensitive sweetie pie" image of men we see in Hollywood and on television these days. I like making fun of these guys, but the truth is that they can teach us something about what it means to be both fully warrior and fully poet. We need the heart and voice of a poet to woo women, care for children, and dance with life. And for many years, I sucked at it.

When I got out of the military, this became even more clear. I did not know how to connect to civilian life at all, having lost touch with so much of what makes life worth living. This just would not work, I realized, and so I threw myself into the mission of reintegrating into civilian life: going back to college, joining a good church, and making some friends. My goal was to find a wife and settle into "happily ever after," but this was easier said than done. To this day, some of my college friends will still recount with smiles what a bull in a china shop I was in those days: wildly intense, trying hard and failing miserably, not realizing what a brute I was. Slowly, though, I realized I could not relate to those around me.

I left the Army as a noncommissioned officer and enlisted in college as a private first class. I began to study civilians and strategically made efforts to become one of them. As silly as that sounds, I knew I didn't fit into this world and needed to relearn how to do so if I wanted to live a full life. So, I got a job at a local smoothie shop, making coffee and other blended beverages, which was the most college-civilian thing I could think of. My wife still laughs about this, thinking of that image: a GI Joe disguised as a barista, fooling no one.

This was when I met my wife, and here's how it happened in her own words:

> John blows into town one day and turns our college world upside down. Riding a Harley, sporting a full and threatening beard, it was immediately obvious he was a man fresh from war. The guys wanted to be him (including my then boyfriend). The girls wanted to date him (except me!). And he quickly became what seemed like the center of our big group of friends. Whenever we'd go out to eat, he'd buy everyone's meal. Whenever we wanted to meet up, he'd invite everyone to his home—that he owned. He was head-and-shoulders above us in life experience and still paid us the compliment of wanting to be friends. What he lacked in experience, he found in assimilating into our group of friends, eventually smoothing out the edges of his Ranger sense of humor.
>
> College John still had his flaws, including occasionally making girls cry with his straightforwardness and wearing all one color—like a beige T-shirt with khaki shorts and Birkenstocks. All. One. Color. He was trying, though, demonstrating how inclusive he was, willing to hang out with anyone, while decorating his side tables with his grandmother's doilies. He was getting better at transitioning from War John to Student John. It must have been a hard adjustment from hanging with a squad of burly men for years to then sitting in philosophy class and attending campus ministries with people who seemed fragile and thin-skinned compared to those in his time overseas; nevertheless, he came out on top and won the hearts of everyone.

He even once invited our group to his parents' home on the coast and gave a sort of leadership training for the weekend among pool parties and grilling out. Now, I laugh out loud thinking about that. I attended a seminar at his house? Who was this guy? He was definitely weird for the average college student. I hoped one of his girlfriends could fix him. Alas, they did not. But eventually our marriage showed him how the tough-guy persona wasn't the only thing I needed from him. And when he saw that, he began to change, but it was definitely not an overnight thing.

John was struggling, but not from being a lost cause or due to his arrogance as I had wrongly thought. He was just confident, assured of himself and his experiences (which were way more than any of us had by then). He also had the wrong first impression of me as shallow and flighty. We were not very impressed with each other for over a year. After one real conversation, though, the rest was history. Our romance was like fireworks—fast and bright—and we were married within months.

Then, the real work began. We had to work hard—really hard—to become what the other needed in a spouse. We both had so much to offer yet so much to change before we could. With his former tough-guy bravado and my man-eater controlling type, we were rescued from what could have ended up an absolute train wreck. God moved mightily in our marriage as we submitted to Him, and this has sustained us ever since: leaning on Him and making each other a priority. That's how we changed. That's how we've built the strong marriage we have now. We saw that the dance needed different steps. We changed, because we had to. We learned new moves. And we're still dancing in the moonlight (our favorite song).

TOUGH GUYS DESTROY BEAUTIFUL THINGS

For most of my adult life now, I've been in tough-guy circles, and there is a common thread I see in these groups. A tough guy tends to ruin relationships, often without even meaning to do so. I personally don't want to fall prey to that temptation, so I try to protect myself and loved ones from my kind's tendency to destroy beautiful things. I like having a wife! I like having children who look up to me and don't resent me. I like my "normal" life, and I want to keep it.

I have studied the men who unconsciously dismantle their lives with their toughness, looking for warning signs to be aware of. One sure sign I see in most men who don't know how to keep "nice things" in their life, like the tenderness of a woman and the innocence of children, is their own rigidity. They're just so inflexible with life, and as a result, when things change, stuff breaks. If you don't want this to be you, you've got to dance a little more, finding the right balance in each and every moment. But first, you have to be aware of the warning signs that destroy the beautiful things in your life. Here is a list of what I've noticed.

EMOTIONAL DISTANCING

We're so busy being tough guys that we forget that a major part of being a man is wooing the wife and showing affection to the kids. Sure, our loved ones need us to be strong and capable defenders against danger. But in reality we run a greater chance of sabotaging our relationships than we do of having a hundred ninjas suddenly invade our homes.

We need to be strong but we also need to love our families with real affection. Some men are too much Warrior and not enough Poet, and somewhere along the line we got the idea that men are supposed to be solid oaks that are stoic and strong but kind of lifeless. That's no good.

Eventually, our emotional distance is going to wither away the affections of our bride. And our kids, who may appreciate our strengths and grow to respect us in some ways, may secretly never love us because they are afraid. This could grow into outright resentment as they are damaged by the love and connection they feel was robbed from them. This is unacceptable. We cannot afford to be failures here. Have the courage to be open and vulnerable, no matter how silly it seems and no matter how uncomfortable it feels. Suck it up and do it, because it's the right and loving thing to do; and over time, it will get easier.

SHORTSIGHTEDNESS

We're so busy taking over the world that we can't see anything else. But you and I are more than how many people we could kill in 2.4 seconds. We are more than our body counts or thousand-yard stares or ammo caches and weapons arsenals. Our identity isn't wrapped up in just what we can do, so quit being so busy taking over the world and notice your family. There's more to life than doomsday prepping, fantasy football, golf, work, and drinking beer. Trust me.

From my family is part of where I get my will to fight. I love my wife and boys. I love other people's families, as well. I am committed to serving them and even trading my life for theirs, if it comes down to that. But my will to fight is fed through the love and affection I have for people, God, and country. I don't want to be so busy trying to prepare myself for some unknown enemy or become the next "big name" in the firearms industry that I miss what's right in front of me. This is the job of the Poet: to appreciate life as it is right now, to see the wonder of it all and relish what you have, knowing that nothing lasts forever. There is more to life than just being a tough guy.

TRYING TO BE RIGHT

I don't think most fights I've had in my marriage have been worth it. Yes, we need to fight stuff out, and disagreements can be healthy when done the right way. But that's the thing: I've fought with my wife too many times the *wrong* way. You know what I mean—something starts you off, and then there's a disagreement, then a misunderstanding, then voices raise; and before you know it, you're sleeping on the couch because you compared her to her mother. Once the fog lifts and some time marches on, I get a little perspective and approach my wife with an apology and a much more constructive way to rehash our disagreement. We got into a battle royale in the first place, however, because I wanted to be right.

My wife's done the same thing many times, but that's her business. My point is that it's not a male problem—it's a human problem and one I've definitely struggled with. Far too many relationships fail only to have one person look back in regret, thinking to themselves, "I wish I hadn't tried to make a point all the time." Back off, smile, say you're sorry for your part—and mean it. There are, of course, times when you really do need to duke it out, but that's a freakishly small amount of the time.

DANCING WITH WISDOM

After getting married, I realized I was going to have to learn how to communicate differently with my wife than I did with my buddies. It's still a process, but it all started with recognizing I sucked at it. But this is how learning happens: by first recognizing our own ignorance. Life is not the way you want it to be, soldier; and if you go through the world with this fixed idea of how things should be, you're going to miss a lot. Don't do that.

A real man knows how to dance with whatever life throws at him. This doesn't make him weak or soft or less of a warrior. In fact, one of the greatest warriors who ever lived was a dancer. King David from the Bible danced with all his might—to the point that it even embarrassed his wife. He didn't care, though; he was willing to put himself out there, appearing undignified, clumsily flailing around for what really matters.

Although he was a famously celebrated warrior, David was an equally passionate poet. His heartfelt musings and prayers to God make up a majority of the book of Psalms in the Bible. He stacked bodies and poured out his heart to God for himself, his family, and his kingdom. This man learned the hard way what inflexibility will get you, and as he grew older and wiser, he became more compassionate. His heart opened and softened to the point that he hesitated to punish an insubordinate son who challenged his authority and threatened the security of the kingdom.

David knew that life was a dance and that if you were going to make your way through it, you'd better learn some moves. His artist's heart helped him lead and love better, and to this day he is revered for such qualities. He was someone not just surviving on a limited set of skills and emotions but thriving as a whole person—embracing the many facets of both defender and lover of people. He was a man of letters, a writer and musician, a political leader and warrior. He danced and sang and was one heck of a Casanova (which got him into trouble early in life). He lived life wholeheartedly and led well. He wasn't a perfect man, full of flaws like the rest of us, but he understood that to live fully, he had to marry his heart and his mind. He had to learn to dance, and so do we.

PRACTICUM

Why are you even reading this practicum?

It's obvious, dude: Go dancing. This isn't metaphorical. Get out on the dance floor and move! Get out of your comfort zone.

Write a love poem to your muse and share it with her.

Open up about something that's weighing on your heart to a family member you've been emotionally closed off to.

Do something to open your heart and teach yourself the importance of balancing your rough edges with practices that make you a little gentler.

Stop being a prick.

Learn to flex with life and love. Others are counting on it.

8

Goodness, Not Greatness

He has told you, O man, what is good; and what does the Lord require
of you but to do justice, and to love kindness, and to walk humbly
with your God?

—MICAH 6:8

Michael Faustus stood triumphantly before the peak
of South America's tallest mountain. As a businessman who had grown weary of the boardroom,
Faustus plunged headlong into grueling adventures. He had visited every continent, seen the wonders of the world, run with
the bulls in Spain, and even traversed the English channel.

As his achievements multiplied, an odd thing happened to
this man. He became more and more possessed by further
achievement; he wanted more. Bigger. Better. Greater. People
his age were winding down, but he was more restless now than

when he was a young executive in his thirties. No matter what he did, he could not find the satisfaction he sought.

In the final few feet of Faustus's climb up Mount Aconcagua, he paused a moment before pressing on to the summit. Knowing the moment of victory was nearly upon him, he wanted to be ready to revel in his success so that he could squeeze every ounce from the experience. As his gloved hand grasped the very last icy hold, he pulled himself up over the ledge atop the peak of human achievement. There, literally looking down on the rest of the world, he was surprised by what he found.

For the middle-aged mountaineer, he was not greeted by enlightenment at the end of his greatest accomplishment. No inner peace found him there among the clouds. Instead, there was just . . . nothing. No fanfare. No joy. No sense that he was any different from the man who stood at the base of the mountain days earlier. In contrast, he felt lonelier than ever before as he searched the horizon, wondering what his mission would be *now*.

What would he put his hand to next? There was nothing left. No more mountains to climb. Nowhere else to go—but down.

He squinted and turned a complete circle, his heartbeat quickening and a lump forming in his throat. *Was this it?* Faustus hunched slightly, bracing against the brutally cold winds. A sense of dread that began from some place deep inside was growing in his stomach and spreading to his limbs. It became hard to swallow. Worried he was going to have a panic attack, he fought to control his breathing and focus on the beauty around him.

"Peace," he said, quietly coaching himself. But there was no peace. With more wealth, respect, and fame than a man could hope for, he had all he had ever wanted. Despite everything, though, he was miserable and worse off than ever before. There was nothing left to strive for, no higher summits. Here at the top of the world, hope had fled like a thief in the night. He thought: *Did I really trade my very soul for this?*

Through the silence, a sinister wind seemed to hiss: "Yes."

THE MEASURE OF A MAN

The above story is and is not true. It has not happened to the fictitious man Michael Faustus, but it is happening to mankind everywhere. Faustus could have made his life about relationships or service or even committing to a greater cause beyond himself, but instead he chased after the vainglorious idols of status, money, power, and accomplishments that ultimately don't satisfy.

Every man wants to be "great" in the sense that others think much of him, respect him for his achievements, and marvel at his success. I get it. I've been there, too, and there's nothing wrong with going after things. But while those accomplishments can add to life, they cannot *make* a life. Faustus went after the allure of greatness but remained unaware that real satisfaction comes from goodness.

What does it mean to be great, and where does goodness fit into the equation? I wonder if you can tell the difference between a great man and a good one by the way people act at their funerals. For a great man, the people will come with respect and admiration. They will speak with reverence for what he accomplished. But that's about it.

I imagine a quiet viewing room where two smartly dressed men exchange some hushed comments about the man's net worth. They might muse over how bad the fight will be among those who argue over his estate. But who will weep for such a man? Will his children stand at his funeral with stern faces as they think through the years they were neglected for board meetings and high living? Will his newest young wife mourn for long?

In contrast, when a good man dies, the people weep. They can't help it. The funeral is filled with tears, laughter, and memories. When goodness fades, we are compelled to mourn. It is only natural. Greatness, I'm afraid, does not necessarily engender the same response.

Recently, I overheard two buddies talking about a man who was extremely wealthy, and one said, "Hey, what is he worth?" As they were considering the answer, I butted in, like I sometimes do in these situations. I had been reading a book but was watching the exchange in my periphery. Intense John crept up the back of my spine, grabbed my brain, and turned my head toward them to say, "Well, I hope he's worth more than money."

One responded, "No, I meant—I was just using the common terminology." They're good dudes and I like them, but it irritates me when we define a man's worth by monetary means. I mean, really? You're worth only . . . *money*? That's it? What an impoverished way of thinking. As the early church father Augustine said, "Earthly riches are filled with poverty." We have to be careful how we define worth, because we spend our lives pursuing that definition.

Picture a successful person. What do they look like? Do they have a big house, lots of money? Do their kids like them, does their spouse admire them? Are they known in their community as someone who is kind and generous, trustworthy and responsible? Have they left the world better than they found it, or did they squander their lives satisfying their own ego? To achieve anything, we have to know what we're aiming at, and these days we seem so confused about what true success is.

I'm tired of hearing about "great men" who have a huge net worth and already a few divorces under their belt. These men tend to make a lot of money and have a high social status, but are they great? I'm not so sure. Because our culture calls material wealth "great," we are compelled to respect such men, but money doesn't make you honorable.

I don't care if you *do* end up building a rocket ship to Mars or leaving behind a legacy worth billions. If your kids don't know you, then you aren't a very admirable man, at least not in my book. This brand of success is, of course, familiar to the world, but there's so much more to a good life than being able to buy a lot of toys. A man is worth more than what he has and what he makes. A man is worth what he *is*.

MORE THAN GREATNESS

Please, don't get me wrong. I am not anti-achievement. Money can be good, and there's nothing wrong with having goals. Success can be useful in creating a meaningful life, when rightly considered. But there's just so much more to life than being great.

That said, greatness is still a good goal. It just can't be the *only* goal of our lives, or even the primary one. Solely seeking greatness runs me headlong into an unbalanced life, which is ultimately not a success. I want to chase after goodness *while* going after greatness. My aim is to be the best at whatever I do without getting too caught up in the results or neglecting other priorities. We can, after all, have greatness without goodness; and that's not good at all.

What are you going to go after in your life? What lofty goals have you nursed in your heart? Having big dreams is part of what makes a man come alive, and there's nothing wrong with this. We all want to tackle a challenge worthy of our talents and see ourselves succeed. That is all good and natural. As men, we should find something we are good at and go for it—all-out. Just don't stop there. Because it is not enough to merely be great. We have to be good, also.

We all need money to live, and success doesn't hurt our chances of creating a great life. But there's so much more to life than riches. One of my most contented times in life was when I was a broke missionary living abroad with my family. A fan belt on our car would screech whenever we cranked up and accelerated, and our hubcaps would fall off as we drove until we had none left. At that time, we lived week-to-week, having spent our entire life-savings on the mission field, serving one of the greatest causes I've ever participated in. And we were virtually penniless— it was awesome.

What in the world, then, does it mean to be successful? What do you value, and how do you measure your worth? In warring cultures, a concept we are unacquainted with in civilized society, the success of a person was typically wrapped up in how good of a warrior they were. Nowadays, in most of the developed world, we value a person's ability to produce commercially viable goods. We esteem people who either make things that make a lot of money (e.g., Bill Gates and Steve Jobs) or those who *have* a lot of money (e.g., Warren Buffet).

Popularity and attractiveness are prized attributes, as well. Hollywood actors and rock stars adorn the covers of our magazines and dominate our news cycles. We call these people successful, but it is often these same people who overdose, check into rehab, and commit suicide. Life isn't as good at the top as many of us imagine.

Every culture has its own version of success, and a culture's picture of a successful man tells you a lot about that culture. When I lived in Central America, for example, success was based on how good of a soccer player you were. That's what made you a "real" man, at least among the young men I knew.

In America, which is very entrepreneurial, success often comes down to net worth, because most corporations are fueled by a single objective: profit. A high personal net worth is essentially the equivalent of being a profitable company, so it makes sense that we would value people who have a lot of material wealth. Human beings, however, are not corporations and therefore need more than money to fuel a life of meaning and significance.

Every societal definition of success falls short in some sense of defining what a man is worth. Ultimately, no one can tell you what your value is. In some sense, you have to define that for yourself. My personal belief is God gets to decide what a good man is. If He created me, then He gets to define what I'm worth. It just makes sense. So what does He say?

Five times in the New Testament, the different biblical authors talk about "living a life worthy of your calling." I've stood on this phrase for years, and it's served as an anchor for my own search for worth and value. How *do* I live a life worthy of my calling? What *does* it mean to measure up what the Creator of the Universe expects? This is a beckoning to another kind of success, one that goes beyond greatness.

You may not believe what I believe, and that's fine. But we as men are called to sacrifice ourselves for a cause larger than ourselves. And that means we must be not just great, but good. No matter how you slice it, this is a high calling and one that requires discipline and strength. It won't happen by accident.

FIRST THINGS FIRST

The measure of a man comes down to what priorities he sets for himself and how well he balances them. In regard to the question of what a man is worth, a twentysomething will offer a radically different answer from that of a fortysomething. And they should. My grandfather turned ninety recently, and he's answering the question differently from a guy in his thirties who's trying to move up in life. All of this should offer us some perspective on what the "good life" really looks like.

You are going to land in all kinds of unpredictable places in life, doing things you never planned for. When you're young, your vocation often feels like everything, but as you get older, your priorities adjust and you realize your legacy is more than just what you can accomplish. Your worth is found in something deeper: in the lives of your children and loved ones, in the private relationships that have nothing to do with who may remember you a hundred years from now. You may end up broke but full of true riches. Life is an adventure, filled with trials and disappointments, incredible successes and astounding failures—and you are none of these things. You are something more.

For my part, I've decided that faith is my most important priority, so if I crush it in every other area of life but look nothing like Jesus at the end of my life, then that's a failure. Goodness, for me, means trying to be better on a daily basis while recognizing the areas where I fall short and vowing to do better next time. Living a life worthy of my calling means aligning with what matters most and living as close to that as I can. When I act in accordance with my greatest values, life is good. When I don't, trouble is nearby.

Another priority is my marriage. You really have to nail this.

No "happily ever after" happens accidentally, and I've learned that you've got to pour lots of time and intentionality into any important relationship, especially when it comes to a spouse. Your intimate relationships affect you at the deepest level and ripple out into every other area, so you don't want to screw this up. It takes daily focus to make a marriage work, and without it the relationship will die.

The same goes for children. I want my kids to know me and want to spend lots of time making memories with me. Children emulate what we show them, so if I consistently demonstrate that a career is more important than family, what do you think they are going to reflect back to me as they get older? They won't have any time to hang with their old man, because they'll be doing exactly what I taught them. I want to make an impact on the world, but it all starts at home—where my influence is greatest.

I also have to pay the bills, so I'm not shy about admitting I'm going to benefit from working hard. We all need to earn well so that we can be charitable to those in need and be good providers. There is nothing wrong about being great at what you do so that you can take care of the ones you love.

It's also good to want to work on yourself, both physically and mentally. This is another kind of greatness that affects all areas of my life. I want to be a good protector, so I allocate a certain amount of time to training myself to be the best defender possible. But it doesn't end there. I want to be able to serve others. No man is an island, so I want to serve the communities of which

I am a part. I want to love others well and be a force for good in the world, speaking up in the face of injustice and being an all-around good citizen.

All of this requires balance. Some might say that you have to give everything your all, but that just doesn't work. You can't give 110 percent to everything all the time, as I discussed in the last chapter. To maximize one area of my life at the expense of these other key priorities will be counterproductive. If I focus too much on work at the expense of family, or vice versa, I'm cooked. Goodness means knowing what matters most, and managing your priorities and responsibilities accordingly.

Ultimately, the success of a man rests on what values he sets for himself. What is most important to you? How well can you balance those things? You want your priorities to be in harmony with the rest of life so that you can keep the balance going. You don't need to become an idealistic picture of absolute awesomeness. You just need to focus on what you already know you need to do, balancing all of it as best you can.

GOOD IS BETTER THAN GREAT

What *are* we chasing? Greatness sounds ambitious enough, so why *not*? Shouldn't everyone aspire to be great? In antiquity, greatness meant something different from the definition today. Leo the *Great*, Alexander the *Great*, Charles the *Great*. All these men were successful individuals whose greatness seems to be a combination of many things: charisma, heroism, a sharp mind, charity, and so on. They were considered in their time to be larger than life because they were oftentimes the *whole package.*

Many in George Washington's time would have revered him similarly. He was respected and loved as a complete man, not just a successful one. He was certainly not the greatest war captain ever, but he was a good man.

When Washington became commander in chief, his military résumé was an unimpressive combination of blank spots and defeats. Still, he had a "greatness" about him that emanated from an all-around goodness. He was regarded as a man of extremely high moral character, and nearly all who met the general instantly respected him. He had the "smell" of greatness about him. People sensed it. It wasn't one thing; it was the consuming force of his person. Tall and virtuous, he towered over his fellow man in more ways than one.

Today, however, greatness has taken on a different meaning. We are ready to offer such a label to anyone who climbs to the top of his field. Michael Jordan, Sigmund Freud, Steve Jobs, and Tom Cruise have found greatness in their respective times, because they climbed to the very top of a particular game, and the world marveled. They are modern heroes, and many of us are desperate to be one of them.

But what do *you* really know about these men? Are they good people? Did they have good marriages and personal lives? If they had never climbed to the top of their fields, would we still say, "That's a life I want to emulate"? Or perhaps we are only enamored of their celebrity, conflating that with true greatness.

Settling for society's definition of greatness will inevitably leave us empty and alone. Joseph Stalin is certainly a well-known figure from history, but I would not call him great. Still, he had plenty of money, power, and success. The Kardashians are even better known today, but, again, I would not ascribe greatness to this family. They are merely popular. And it is not necessarily "great" to be universally known or even liked.

In previous generations, people wanted to be successful, which they defined as having a good career and family. The modern young person, however, wants fame above nearly everything else. Just *how* many seasons of *American Idol* are there now? How many reality TV shows are created just for the fame-hungry person ready to do anything to make their name known? My, how things have changed.

What is most disheartening about this pursuit is how young people have not done the basic diligence to test whether their goal is worth the cost. Wealth, power, and fame regularly leave their possessors unhappy and wanting more of their drug. Celebrities hit rock bottom in addictions and self-destruction, surrounded by all they could want, and still they often don't wake up to what true happiness is.

People are often consumed by what they seek, then lose everything in their pursuit, only to claim bankruptcy and start the whole process over again, never learning the lesson. I know there are exceptions to all this. But I'm not talking about exceptions. I'm talking about the rule. Some of the richest people I've ever met were miserable and secretly hated by many. We just don't understand the cost of so-called greatness. Rarely is it worth what we have to pay.

It's awesome to climb to the very top of your field. To be the fastest runner in the world is an incredible achievement, as is being the most brilliant mathematician, computer programmer, UFC fighter, or author. Surely, these people are achieving greatness in their work, but is that greatness in life? If you grow an empire only to lose your wife, kids, friends, character, and soul along the way, are you really great? The world might say yes. The masses won't spend a second thinking otherwise. But I can't help but wonder if that's all greatness is.

Personally, I would like to be the fastest gun in the West. Literally. I'd love to earn the moniker of the "most dangerous warrior alive." But if such prestige comes at the expense of what I value most, then no thanks. That's too high of a cost and literally not worth it to me. It'd be like trading dollars for cents. A Faustian exchange for cheap greatness is a hollow victory, and though the crowds may cheer me on, I would know that I was a fraud.

Everywhere we look, we see false heroes: people who have achieved greatness at the cost of their own goodness. Your fate is sealed the moment you set foot on their course. A hero, however, is one whose example awakens your soul. These are the people who drive you to something greater than yourself, something more than just power, wealth, and fame. Truth. Justice. Beauty. These are what catch a soul on fire.

Let me ask you, then: Whose example makes you want to be a better man? Are you filling your life with these stories and images, or are you cluttering it with hollow concepts like "greatness"? To be *truly* great begins, and ends, with goodness.

We must find something inside ourselves that is honorable and true, not just expedient, and aspire to an ideal beyond what we often settle for. The loss of heart of men is too great to risk on simply hoping one day we will get around to preparing ourselves and instilling these values in the next generation. We have a heavy and glorious task ahead of us, and its worth is immeasurable. It won't just be given to us, though. We will have to take this promised land, and it will cost us everything.

GREAT AT WAR, BAD AT LIFE

Robert Rogers was the grandfather of the American Army Rangers. An incredible warrior and tactician, he was well-known in England, America, and France for his exploits in the French and Indian War. In those days, he would have been on par with the likes of Benjamin Franklin—he was *that* well-known and respected.

The problem, however, was that Rogers was terrible with money. He stunk at business and kept getting screwed over, particularly by the Crown, while accruing huge war debts and expecting the "team" to pay his expenses. Then, England would leave him hanging. Creditors chased him his whole life, and because of this he struggled to ever escape survival mode.

Rogers got married but immediately went off to war and barely saw his wife for years. When he returned, they got divorced.

Some historians believe she found out that he got syphilis or some other STD from sleeping around and had just had enough. That may be true, or it may be that she was just tired of being broke and neglected, with creditors showing up at their door. Either way, it makes sense. Rogers's wife never saw him, and there were rumors of his "escapades," so she ended it.

Later in life, he fell into heavy drinking and could never really get ahead or change his position. The man was bad with money and terrible in relationships, but incredible at war.

As we've already seen, this is a legacy that carries through to even the modern soldier: a dangerous force to be reckoned with on the battlefield but a bit of a boy in the rest of life. Warriors are often both tactical geniuses and physical specimens who can endure longer, fight harder, and go faster than the average man. But these same men can't keep a relationship together to save their lives.

Why is this? One reason is we tend to over-index on the "war" part of "Warrior" and under-index on the "poet" side of life, which is most of life that isn't war. However, to be excellent at one part of the formula while neglecting the other is a half-lived life. That's not a whole man, and it's not a full life. Many marriages have been sacrificed on the altar of ambition and paid the price for doing so.

Your career is only part of your calling. It is not the totality of who you are or what you can be. It's good to chase success—to an extent—but a successful career is not worth sacrificing everything for one. To get ahead at work at the neglect of family is to fall behind in life. I do want you to work hard and get lots of nice things to enjoy. So, hurray for ambition. I also want you to feel good about the work you do and your place in the world.

But let's be honest: your hard work is not permanent. Even if you end up inventing a cure for cancer, it will all eventually blow away. In a hundred years, no one will likely know or even care who you were and what you did. Same for me. But our relationships leave a legacy that carry us to the end of this life and into the next. That's the stuff that matters. If you're great at war and bad at relationships, it's time to refocus.

I meet many men who say they want to achieve great things, but they don't understand the cost. "If I can bring my wife and kids along for the journey, that would be great," they say, "so long as they don't get in the way." They don't typically say that second part, but I can tell that's what they mean. And, dude, that is a recipe for disaster. The world worships vocational success far more than a vibrant, growing marriage; but only one of those will contribute to long-term fulfillment.

I'm not saying you should be some kind of free spirit with no direction. Most men want more than that. We want to hold both the ambition of the Warrior and the love of the Poet in healthy tension: to have big dreams and desires alongside a committed reverence for the people we love. Wanting to achieve and accomplish is good; we just want to direct our ambition at something good. If we get this wrong, we miss a lot.

DON'T BE A DUMB BRUTE

We were broke. No money. Worse than "no money"—we were in debt, and my wife and I were fighting again. The same scene played out a hundred times that year. She didn't like being talked to *that* way, and I didn't like the snide remarks or feeling nagged. I would hurt Rebekah's feelings, and she wouldn't appreciate how hard I was working.

The fights would start the same way every time. The details may have been a little different, but it was the same stupid fight over and over. Something would irritate me, I would respond like a brute, then she'd be hurt and attack me. We would go back and forth until my rage peaked and I stormed out of the room.

Sometimes, we'd let our fights last for days, emotionally closed off and ignoring each other. I'm embarrassed to admit it now, but that was a common occurrence in those early days of our marriage. For some reason, it felt strong to not cave. *She's the crazy one who started this*, I would think, not knowing that every dumb brute says the same.

Sure, she may have been partly at fault, but if you call yourself a leader in your marriage, then the lion's share of fault lies with you, always. More often than not, men are the ones who create and sustain the conflict—therefore, we have the power to end it. A woman may bring up something, but it is the man who can keep it going or shut down. And in those days, I kept it going.

Rage felt strong to me; still does, sometimes. The adrenaline coursing through my veins made me feel powerful, invincible even. But a weak man is one who cannot keep his anger in check. There is such a thing as good anger, but it is meant to break down injustices and wrongdoings, not excuse childish behavior. Anger is a tool that should be harnessed on rare occasions to protect the innocent, not put your loved ones in harm's way. When you cannot control your anger, your brutality will likely leave you alone.

To be good, you must become—and stay—utterly humble. Then, you have to do what you don't want to do, which is often going headlong into whatever battle you want to run away from. You have to face your greatest fear, whether it's turning over in the middle of the night and having that hard conversation or admitting to your child you are wrong. You have to confront your boss and political leaders or anyone else when they don't do what's right. This isn't easy. It requires a kind of strength we don't often see, and this is why it's needed.

For much of my life, I have been looking for a man whose example I could follow. In my personal life, I saw many who were feminized by our culture, weak in every area of their lives for the sake of political correctness and cultural acceptance. This did not seem honorable, nor worthy of aspiration. I was also disappointed in the one-dimensionality often found in the "tough-guy crowd." I saw men who either didn't know how to harness their anger for good or blew up at the slightest sign of distress.

Over time, I've learned to not let anger rule me. I've grown in my own ability to work through tough times with my wife and loved ones. It hasn't been easy, and if greatness were my only aim, I never would have taken the time to be good. This work takes a little patience, whether you lean to the "dumb brute" extreme or that of the "nice guy." Either one is not good.

Yes, we are called to strength, but that includes gentleness and self-control. It means being more than nice or unpredictably angry. We have to do better. No one wants to be another Michael Faustus, standing at the top of their greatest achievement, wondering what it was all for. Take the time to be good, and trust the process it takes to get there.

FINDING A NEW MISSION

The soldier who doesn't have a new cause to fight for is going to start drifting, and purposelessness is death to the masculine soul. A lot of wartime trauma is at least exacerbated if not caused by a man's inability to find a new purpose.

Those who suffer from unhealed PTSD, in many cases, are really struggling with finding a new mission in life. When a warrior doesn't have a new challenge to tackle, he is reduced to punching holes in walls—or worse. A man needs a mission that goes beyond himself and his ambitions, if he wants to be good. Without something to anchor us, over time, we end up reliving our old glory days, replaying scenes from a more intense season of life.

Why does this happen? These same men who faced some of the most gruesome and grisly situations in life are now living mundane lives that do not inspire their warrior spirit. When their mind wanders, as it always does, they find it easier to go back to those old experiences. This is what we sometimes call trauma, but really it's often a man's lack of creativity and resolve to find the next battle. And there is always another battle.

Trauma is a real thing and ought to be dealt with. Depending on its level of severity, you will want to seek professional help, but there is only so much you can clean up by focusing on the past. Every man who is living for something greater than himself is oriented toward the future. We all need something to look forward to.

What does the soldier have to look forward to when he comes home if the civilian world is unwilling to care for him in the way that he cares for it? Not much. Anger is the natural response. As is the pull back to adventure, wherever he can find it. And if there is no imminent conflict, he just might have to create it. Think of *First Blood*, where Sylvester Stallone plays John Rambo, a Vietnam vet who has brought the war home and is just itching for an excuse to wage battle on anyone.

When a soldier doesn't fully reintegrate into society, he cuts himself off from those who would support him. He needs a new mission and a team. Yes, there will be those who are bad eggs, even in the civilian world, those who are soft and weak and even despicable. But these people can still teach you things. The weak ones in your life are simply weak in ways you are not. What the soldier fails to appreciate is those same civilians may be stronger in ways that he doesn't yet fully understand. You have a lot to learn from these so-called normal people, and it would do you well to get off your high horse.

When I speak of "soldiers," I'm not talking about just those who have left an actual wartime scenario or who were enlisted in military service, but certainly those men, too. I am also talking about the dude who sees every scenario in life as a do-or-die situation, who can't get over his past and is still stuck in whatever fight he last won. Whether it's the high school football game or your career as a police officer, you've got to move on. There is a battle in front of you that you refuse to face. And because of this denial, you are already losing.

Men tend to find something they're good at, optimize for success, then relive those greatest accomplishments over and over for the rest of their lives until they keel over. Their greatest hope is that people say nice things about them after they become worm food. Sometimes, because they're living too small a life, they invent threats. This is not true greatness. It's not even goodness.

The battlefield has changed. The good old days are gone. Your trophies are rusted, and your medals won't save you. There is a war to be won, and the enemy is vicious—and you're still talking about being a high school football captain? Really? It's time to open your eyes and wake up. Give up your own greatness for the hope of being good, and you'll reap rewards in this life and the next.

PRACTICUM

What are your top ten priorities?

I mean, really. Try to be as honest as possible. List them on a piece of paper as they come to mind. Now, off to the side of each priority, write down what percentage of your time you devote to that priority every day or week.

This exercise sucks, because it forces you to face the fact of your own selfishness and laziness.

People who put "God" as their top priority may see that they spend only a couple minutes per day praying, proving that priority number four— work, for example—takes the vast majority of time. Maybe your kids are priority number three, but you really spend only thirty minutes per day with them, at best.

Or maybe you claim your marriage as priority number two, but don't spend any significant time with her on a daily basis. At best, you sit beside your wife for a couple hours at night, scrolling on your phone before bed. That is not the same as looking into her eyes and listening to what she has to say.

After destroying your naive and incorrect priority list, write out your priorities as they really are. Get real about how you're actually spending time, then contrast it with how you'd like to spend it.

Then, make the necessary adjustments to right the ship. It's humbling, but it's worth it.

9

Raise Little Poets

[F]airy tales do not give the child the idea of the evil or the ugly; that is in the child already, because it is in the world already . . . The baby has known the dragon intimately ever since he had an imagination. What the fairy tale provides for him is a St. George to kill the dragon.

—G. K. CHESTERTON

Childhood now is nothing like it used to be. I grew up in the woods. As a kid, I'd disappear for hours into the tree line, spending most of the day building forts, swimming in lakes, and making up games with my friends. At eight years old, I would spend massive amounts of time outside exploring on my own, completely alone, never bored.

Today, the school year is longer, both parents work, and

children are constantly in front of screens. Spending hours outside running and playing and riding bikes has become a thing of the past, it seems, sadly something of antiquity. As my wife and I have moved an incredible twelve times in fifteen years of marriage, we've noticed that whatever our address is, kids just don't go outside like they used to.

Seven years ago, my wife and I determined the best thing for our kids would be for Rebekah to stay home and homeschool them, but that would mean we'd be a single-income family. Frankly, we didn't make enough money to live on my salary alone and maintain our lifestyle, so we made a tough decision to move out of the house we were renting and into a sprawling apartment complex. We were strapped for cash, and this sacrifice would allow us to still support our primary values. It wasn't easy, but it had its benefits and lessons.

We made the best of this season, believing we'd be able to meet a bunch of young families who would share the complex's many amenities. We were continually shocked that almost no kids used the playground. We went on walks frequently, hoping to connect with people in the neighborhood, but no one seemed to ever go outside. We saw evidence that many children lived right on top of us, but it seemed they were just inside playing video games and watching TV.

Apparently, this is normal.

Nowadays, kids sit still at school for hours every day, trying to fit the mold of what a "good student" should be. Sports and extracurriculars are taking what precious free time used to be left for family dinner, replacing it with nonstop practices and weekend-long activities. While I love and value the role of competitive sports in the development of children, there needs to be time for families to make memories and transfer real-world lessons from parents to the next generation.

Often, our families are in constant hurry mode, our kids are rushed into growing up, and life shows no signs of slowing down. Even the youngest among us are shuttled into more and more "programs" at the tender age of three or four for the sake of "not falling behind." What are we really afraid of missing out on? Family time, skills learned at home, and shared values are irreplaceable investments that we think we'll offer someday only to turn around and see our kids have already grown up.

How do we raise young Warrior Poets in an age of distraction? If we are seeing our kids only for an hour or so a day before they fall into homework or a screen, can it be said that we're really raising them at all? Or is someone else?

Big Tech is happy to instill all kinds of programmed responses in our children through never-ending content and entertainment. The school system, which is run by the state, seems happy enough to fill their time for us, as well. It is only us parents who are too quick to give up control. Why have we stood still while all this has happened, instead of considering what we've lost in allowing institutions to raise and educate our children? It's time we took some power back.

THE MISEDUCATION OF OUR YOUTH

In America especially, we are seeing something happen to our kids. Our children and young adults are becoming mindless drones, victims of a politically correct educational system and a culture that prizes comfort over virtue. In the past twenty years, ADHD diagnoses alone have more than doubled with the prevalence of accidental or "unnecessary" ingestion of the medication increasing by more than 60 percent.[*] We are medicating our children and exposing them to more medications at home more than ever before. Kids are bored, and instead of giving them an outlet for their boredom and creativity, we are drugging them.

Maybe all this is just coincidence or accident, but it sure does look suspicious to me. What benefit does society get from killing a child's love for life and adventure? They become an adult that is easier to control. In the words of Anthony Esolen, "If we can but deaden the imagination, then, we can settle the child down, and make of him that solid, dependable, and inert space-filler in school and, later, a block of the great state pyramid."

In other words, if you can get a kid to stop dreaming, you can get him to conform to an authoritarian system without even knowing it. It makes perfect sense to me that state schools would want to raise good little cogs in the machine rather than the

---

[*] Source: Michael Davidovitch et al., "Challenges in Defining the Rates of ADHD Diagnosis and Treatment: Trends over the Last Decade," *BMC Pediatrics* 17, no. 218 (2017), https://doi.org/10.1186/s12887-017-0971-0.

bold and independent thinkers you and I would like to send out into the world. Esolen continues in his book *Ten Ways to Destroy the Imagination of Your Child*, "Contemporary life happens within walls; for the first time in the history of the human race, most people will spend most of their lives indoors. . . . Children no longer play because we have taken from them the opportunity and, I'll insist, even the capacity to play." This is a tragedy, one that needs to be stopped immediately.

Today's kids aren't making forts and finding bugs, spending hours outside doing non–adult-run activities. They're not exploring or creating much of anything; they're consuming an endless barrage of shows and videos, attending countless activities where they are told what to do and how to do it. During the school year, they may spend hours on homework each evening, which is not necessarily a good thing.

As I look back on my most formative years, I'm aware that the most important stuff I learned wasn't in the classroom. My essential life lessons came from the wrestling mat and from working jobs from the ages of twelve to eighteen. The lessons came from listening to my dad conduct business and deal with his customers and employees, and through learning how to drive a stick shift, run a forklift, pay bills, save money, and work through disagreements. These things forged me. I didn't learn sales, leadership, romance, theology, or taxes from school. I didn't learn to live or how to die from a classroom. And those things matter.

There is schooling, and then there is education, and those are not the same thing. Education is what we are after for our children, which means the classroom has a part to play, but the most critical stuff often happens outside of school. Have we carved out the time with our kids to pass on what we know and who we are? Or are we abdicating our responsibility to educate our youth, because we are just as busy as they are and therefore have to outsource to the so-called experts?

What is happening to our children? In his eye-opening book *Boys Adrift*, Leonard Sax explores why this cultural shift is occurring, and one reason is the relatively new phenomenon of the helicopter parent. These parents are raising boys under their thumb that, in turn, become even more dependent, submissive, and muted instead of wilder and freer. We are not raising young conquerors but sheep who do not know how to think for themselves. I find this at best troubling and at worst absolutely deplorable. We have to fight for the souls of our youth.

Great things come from discipline; and yet, a disciplined young person seems harder to find these days. We have more opportunities and greater advantages than ever, but the commitment to achieve a goal seems almost archaic when youth are more interested in their entertainment updates than in something that's never been done before.

As the great education critic and philosopher Mortimer J. Adler said, "True freedom is impossible without a mind made free by discipline." So, perhaps the reason our society is allowing so many freedoms to be stripped away is because we've been unable to submit to real discipline. There is too much mind-numbing, unconstructive play and not enough of the right kind of work;

worse still, children are not able to pull themselves away from addictive technology. If our kids don't feel the weight of what is most important in life, how can we ever expect them to fight for it?

All this sounds dire, and it is, but the solution is far from complicated. We've got to start walking some of the ancient paths again. There is wisdom in the past that knows how to raise kids better. Our first war for the future begins before we leave the house. That's where freedom comes from and where every revolution begins.

What *does* it mean to train our children in the art of war without robbing them of their innocence? How *do* we teach our young ones that freedom is something worth fighting for? It is not enough to become bold men of action, committed to a higher purpose; we have to teach the next generation to do the same. I'm not claiming I've cracked the code on this, by the way. I'm still working to become a better dad. I have some ideas and think my wife and I have figured out a few things, but the jury is still out on who our kids will become. What I do know, however, is that what society is offering them is just not cutting it. I want my children to be more than mindless drones, tossed back and forth by the latest authoritarian opinion from the government or media. I want them to fight for freedom.

REVOLUTION STARTS AT HOME

One of the best things we did for our family was move out of the suburbs and onto a plot of land where our kids can spend most of their time outside, wandering the woods, building forts, and using their imaginations. I know not everyone can do something like this in the current season of life they are in, and I am not opposed to suburban or even urban living, but I believe that kids should not spend all their time sitting indoors or endlessly moving from activity to activity.

As parents, we are responsible for providing structure for our kids so they have some direction in life and can learn to walk before they run. But we also want to give them enough freedom to fail and grow. In our home, my boys do chores every morning, they eat breakfast, spend two to three hours homeschooling, then go off to explore, catch crickets, shoot BB guns, read, and play with other kids.

In the summer, they swim nearly every day and create new games constantly. When they aren't outside cutting trails with our Belgian Malinois in tow or ranging chickens, they are drawing pictures of dragons and writing adventure stories. They spend a lot of their time with us, and we wouldn't have it any other way. We are raising our own kids—not the state or a screen.

Our children are not completely left to their own devices, but they do experience a tremendous amount of freedom within good boundaries; they've embarked on some cool adventures, both on foot and in their minds. When I'm able to pull away from work, we ride ATVs or horses together.

Each night (unless I'm traveling), I read them a story. Whether it's illustrated Shakespeare plays abridged for children, one of the Great Illustrated Classics, Greek myths, the Green Ember book series, or the Chronicles of Narnia, we are always getting into some new and imaginary tale.

As I read, I do the different character voices, and my wife chimes in with sound effects. Side note to my fellow fathers: read to your kids and don't wimp out on the voices. This is good fun and constantly causes our kids to fall more and more in love with reading every day.

As evidence of this, once we are done reading to our kids and it's time for them to go to bed, they have just one burning question: "How many chapters can we have?" If we say they can read two chapters in bed, they'll be happy, but if I say four they are elated and hug us and shower us with happy thank-yous. They love to read and see it as a gift. It's no exaggeration to say that my eight-year-old has read more than most graduating high schoolers. My kids read *that* much.

This is not a new phenomenon we've stumbled upon. It's old knowledge and timeless wisdom. Ever since human beings were able to read, people have understood that accumulating knowledge naturally puts a child at an advantage to his peers. In our family, we've created a culture of reading, and it's paying off in huge dividends. My belief is this will make our children more knowledgeable, sure, but also freer thinkers, less likely to be pushed around by authority figures who don't have their best interests at heart.

One of my favorite parenting authors is John Rosemond, who says in his classic work *Parenting by the Book* that our nation has been overrun by "experts" for childhood, what he calls the

PPP: "Postmodern Psychological Parenting." This has done incredible harm in just two generations by dispensing rotten and backward thinking that is shaping the lives of our children and the future of our nation. He writes:

> By the mid-1970s, Grandma's common sense had been all but drowned out by the shouts of people with capital letters after their names, who claimed that not only did Grandma not really know what she was talking about (she hadn't gone to college after all), but she also had been dispensing advice that was bad for the psychological health of children. America's parents were now in thrall to Postmodern Psychological Parenting (PPP), an anomalous hybrid of three historically antagonistic schools of psychological thought: Freudian, humanistic, and behavioral. . . .
>
> . . . When [PPP] began gaining a toehold in our culture, every single indicator of positive well-being in America's children has been in a state of precipitous decline. . . .
>
> . . . In just one fifteen year period, from 1980 to 1995, the suicide rate for boys ages ten to fourteen almost doubled! . . .
>
> I grew up in the 1950s. Ironically, my peers and I were expected to shoulder more responsibilities than are kids today, and our parents and teachers expected a lot more of us than is the case today, yet we were much happier than are today's kids.

We have to face the facts. We must realize how we got into this position to fight our way out. The world will tell you that you are perfect just the way you are, and it is a beautiful thought—sort of. The only problem is it is utter horse crap. We have lied to our children and to ourselves about our true nature, and this is costing us far more than we realize.

The more discerning person will realize they can improve immensely. You aren't perfect as you are because you (and I) could be more moral, harder working, in better shape, kinder, more selfless, more educated, and so on. This self-esteem-boosting lie is a stark contradiction to the Book of Jeremiah (17:9), which says, "The heart is deceitful above all things, and desperately sick; who can understand it?" That artificially boosted self-esteem we give kids will likely morph into a self-centered narcissism, so we must be careful.

Our kids, in thinking they are special without working through any rites of passage, are held back from meeting and overcoming real challenges. Children, I think, would be healthier if they were allowed to struggle a little more. If we let them learn to fail and get back up again, they'd be stronger and more resilient than if we continue to insulate them from hardship and keep handing out participation trophies.

RAISING WARRIORS

My oldest son is on a soccer team coached by another parent. He is younger and smaller than most of the kids on the team. My son is outmatched on that field, but there is one saving grace he can cling to, one simple mindset he can has that others likely do not possess: my boy doesn't play soccer; he wages war.

He's playing by the rules, but he fearlessly goes for the ball, driving headlong into a gaggle of bigger boys. He gets knocked down constantly but springs back up to his feet and keeps going. By the end of the game, he is beet red and sweatier than any kid in sight. And I, his father, am grinning ear to ear. This is what I've been trying to build as a parent—a kid who works hard—so please allow me a quick brag about what happened at a recent game.

A group of boys were battling for the ball in front of the opponent's goal. The ball rolled toward the other team's sweeper, who had already wound up for a huge kick and let it fly. The ball shot ten feet across the field and slammed into my son's face. As soon as it happened, I heard the parents beside me gasp. Every kid on the field froze for a moment in shock and pity, but my son—warrior that he is—didn't hesitate. The ball bounced off his face, fell to his feet, and he dribbled forward to score a goal while the entire crowd watched in stunned silence.

Had you been there on the field that day, you would have seen an ecstatic father celebrating his son with such passion that I had to issue an apology to the other parents. This was not talent that scored that goal; it was grit. And I was proud. Sadly, many boys never learn this; they never acquire such drive from their dads. Instead they're scooped up by a nurturing mother who means well but isn't equipped to prepare them for a harsh world. We need mothers to keep our boys alive, and we need fathers to make them hard to kill. Because a boy who is coddled does not grow up to be a good, strong man. He doesn't know how to be a warrior, because no one ever showed him.

When a man lacks a model of strength and steadiness, his only option is to do whatever his buddies are doing. If I'm describing you, I understand. When we don't have someone to show us the way, what else can we do but just kind of drift along, going with the flow? Many of us did not receive the masculine gifts every son is owed by his father, so we just wander. Many men never develop these essential masculine qualities, and as a result we find ourselves today in a crisis.

We have lost what it means to be a man.

While growing up, many boys who are now men did not have an ideal dad or even a father figure who was around. This can damage a guy in more ways than one, leaving a mark on future generations. The good news is it's not too late, and there is hope for change. As a father myself, I can see how difficult it is to raise a son right, to become a whole man and teach my boys what true masculinity is. But as I learn more, I share those lessons with them.

Flawed man that I am, by the grace of God, I'm growing, often two steps forward and one back. But make no mistake about it: that's improvement happening. We all mess up, but any man who continues to learn from his failures is headed in the right direction.

When I was a kid, before each of my soccer games my dad would take me through a kind of mental preparation, teaching me to focus on the goal in front of me. He would turn off his car as we arrived in the parking lot and ask me to close my eyes. Then he'd say, "OK, son. Picture yourself winning. You are lightning fast. No one can keep you from scoring. You are unstoppable. You are fearless."

On and on he would go until my mind was focused and I was ready to go out on the field and be a terror. I wasn't always the best player, but I would put more heart and strength into that game than any other kid. I would work harder, and that hard work made me better. I grew into the mindset my dad gave me. I took this strategy and shared it with my own children when I became a father, and you have already seen the effect in their lives. I appreciate my dad, because he taught me to focus and work hard, which is a big part of being a man. Grit, discipline, focus, aggression—these are tools every man needs. And if we can learn them in boyhood, we're better off.

TRAINING POETS

One of my deepest desires as a man is to do everything I can to be the best father possible. A scene from *Braveheart* haunts my memory, where young William Wallace has just lost his father and his Uncle Argyle is taking him under his care. The boy's father has been killed in battle, and the young Wallace picks up his dad's sword and holds it, enthralled. His uncle notices this and snatches the blade out of the boy's hands, saying, "First, learn to use . . . this," pointing to the young man's head, "then I'll teach you to use . . . this," motioning to the weapon.

You could write volumes about what an awesome lesson in parenting this is. That's what it means to raise a man. That's it, all of it: teach a boy to use his head—and his heart—before you teach him to fight, and you've given him a gift most men never receive. We must let our children become poets before requiring them to become warriors. We must teach them innocence, then wisdom, and then war.

To be a father is a constant exercise in humility, as the process of raising a child forces you to face the demons of your past and wrestle them. You must get what you may not have received in childhood so that you can pass it onto your own kids. Then, you have to properly guide them through each phase of life, from dependence to independence to taking care of others. It's not an easy job, but it is a noble one.

One way men fail to raise good children is by focusing on only one or two areas in their own lives, like provision and protection, only to fall short in all the others. A good dad isn't just a good provider; he is father, protector, counselor, king, judge, friend, and so many other identities. A boy's dad is his best window into the world of masculinity. So if you want to bring up boys who will become good men, you have to go first—because you can't give what you don't have.

One of the best things you can do for your kids is be there. The statistics for children raised in single-parent homes, especially when the father is missing, are absolutely astounding. Just about everything a parent doesn't want for their child—from early sexual experiences to dropping out of school to drug addiction—are all correlated to a lack of a dad at home.

According to Leonard Sax, when young boys grow up without a father figure, it's not the Peter Pan fantasy we might have imagined as children ourselves. It's more of a nightmare. The role of a father in the life of a child cannot be understated. This role is sorely lacking in many cultures, especially ones we dare call "modern" and "civilized."

As Warrior Poets, we need to be good dads. Even if you didn't grow up with a man who had high moral character, a father or mentor who taught you right from wrong and how to focus, you must be better—if not for yourself, then for your children and grandchildren and every future man who will ever spend time with you. The world will be only as great as its men, and we have a lot of bad guys out there. If we want a better world, we need to make better men. It's just that simple. And better men begin with fathers.

I feel great empathy for any man who didn't get everything he needed from his dad. That's true for most men, including myself. Still, this is no excuse. You and I have a responsibility to break our generational patterns and become something better than what was modeled for us. This is not easy, but it is necessary. The stakes are just too high to do otherwise.

BOY BECOMES MAN

As babies, we're taken care of by someone else. We are fed, changed, and fawned over the moment we cry for any need or want that may strike us. We are entirely someone else's responsibility. A shift, however, happens throughout boyhood and adolescence, and we learn to start carrying ourselves a little more; we begin to share the burden. This is how a boy gradually becomes a man.

As teenagers, we get a taste of more independence: we go out with friends, do our chores, dress ourselves, start dating, get a part-time job, learn to make our way in the world. And that brings us to adulthood, which is when we move out, get a place of our own, and learn to stand on our own two feet. But it doesn't stop there. Eventually, many of us end up getting full-time jobs, begin paying bills, get married, buy a house, and start a family. This is when we begin to take control of our lives and learn what it means to be responsible for others. It can also be a stressful time, especially if no one taught you that all of this is good and natural.

That's just what we see in the world today, especially in America. Our current problem is that many men simply refuse to grow up, downright avoiding these necessary rites of passage that teach a man how to carry burdens. Now more than ever, young men are not branching out on their own; if anything, they're only extending adolescence into the first couple decades of adulthood.

Never really willing to be responsible for anyone but themselves, these young men miss out on a lot, staying stuck as boys in men's bodies, scared to take on the burden of responsibility. It's a sad state of affairs, but you see it around you everywhere.

I get it. Nobody likes feeling stressed or burdened by innumerable responsibilities. At least, I don't. But to deny this mantle of responsibility is a rejection of what makes a man a *man*. Men are given strength to help carry the burdens of others. It's what all these gifts we've received from others are for: to enrich the lives of the people around us.

As a man, you are meant to serve not just yourself but to make the world a better, safer place and pay it forward so that others can have the same opportunities you had. Until you realize this, you will remain a boy.

YOUR CHILD AS A TABLE

The basic needs of every human are physical, social, spiritual, and mental. I think of these as the four pillars of a successful life, and this framing has been useful for me as a parent.

We can think of those key pillars as legs on a table, with the table being your child. The goal of this exercise is of course to ensure children are well balanced and capable of supporting the weight the world will later put on them. I don't think any parent, no matter how bad or lazy, wants their kids to be in prison, addicted to drugs, or out on the street. No one wants to see a young person ruin their lives over a few bad decisions, nor do we want them to be social outcasts or to live spiritually bankrupt lives. We want our kids to succeed and thrive. Getting these basics in place helps make that happen.

You need at least four areas to ensure a child has a life that is successful in every sense of the word that matters. You might be able to imagine more legs to make the table even sturdier, but four will do just fine. Chill out, you overachievers, and stop trying to hijack my four-legged-table metaphor! And yes, there are three-legged tables, but they are an abomination and should be broken into splinters and burned. If you have such a table, I will wait as you do the right thing and destroy it.

There's stuff that only men can teach a child, and if a boy is being raised by a single mother, she has her work cut out for her. That is a noble and thankless job. Single moms are heroes and deserve all kinds of praise and support as well as help. As they say, it takes a village to raise a child, and that village better include some men who know what they're doing.

Just like Uncle Argyle raised his orphaned nephew in the film, sometimes we need to depend on extended family and friends to help us raise our children. But make no mistake: it is the role of a man to make a man. Mothers are essential and necessary to the growth of a child, but the job is not complete without a strong masculine presence, especially when it comes to raising boys. So let's examine these needs one at a time.

PHYSICAL NEEDS

First, let's take the physical. This means we're providing healthy food, clothes, medical attention, and all the other stuff our kids need. This is not just about paying the bills but includes taking a more active role to make sure our kids are growing strong and healthy bodies. This is baseline stuff: the lowest tier of existence in which you are keeping another human being alive. This is well and good, but not sufficient for raising a young boy.

Many men stop here, and the result is a boy who never becomes a man, at least not without some serious intervention by other men. So, you may be failing as a dad, but you pat yourself on the back, saying, "I'm paying the bills, aren't I? I gave them this house to live in." Again, understand that this is the lowest form of fatherhood. Please, do this, yes, at the very least. But don't stop there. Children deserve so much more.

Our goal is not to just keep our kids alive. It is to show them how to be a man. Teach your sons to properly work out and push themselves far past where they think their limits are. Teaching discipline and pain management in workouts constitutes some of the most sacred rites of passage we bring our sons through. Teach them to fight. If you don't know how, take some jiu-jitsu or kickboxing classes together.

It's up to us men to teach our sons how to be strong and dangerous and raise them to be forces for good in the world. Yes, this takes extra effort but also happens to be really fun memories you don't want to miss out on. And if that's not motivating enough, do it because one day your kids will probably be taking care of you when you're old and frail. So play nice.

SOCIAL NEEDS

The second leg of the table is the social needs of a child. Meeting social needs is about resolving conflicts. This is "how to win friends and influence people" stuff (the book of the same name by Dale Carnegie is one I highly recommend), which includes having good manners and exhibiting emotional intelligence.

A lot of times, we prize high-IQ people, but they go to work for others who are able to manage their own emotions, resolve conflict, and win over other people. Emotional Intelligence has great advantages over IQ. This is the social aspect of a successful life, and as dads we need to make sure we're cultivating these skills in our boys. They matter.

A child, once he reaches a certain age, needs to be able to stop wiggling, sit still, look someone in the eye, shake their hand, and say something of value. Learning to get along with others is a big part in creating a successful life. This is also the area where we need to teach our boys to control their anger, which doesn't come naturally.

I had an anger problem as a boy. Whenever I didn't get my way, I would become so mad that I would hold my breath until I turned red, then pass out. True story. As a toddler, I'd do this in the grocery store when I didn't get a toy I wanted. I kept this up for a couple years until my mom, in exasperation, turned to my dad for help.

Here's how my father solved the problem. The next time I got angry, my dad pulled me into a separate room and said, "You want to pass out?! Well go ahead and pass out!" I don't remember any instance of me holding my breath and passing out as a kid except the last time I ever did it. I remember holding my breath, seeing the room spin, then hitting the floor. My dad didn't scoop me up and give me my way. He stood by and did, well, nothing. He showed me that my behavior didn't get me what I wanted. I never tried again. Later, he helped me learn how to take deep breaths and count slowly down from ten when I found that my temper was flaring out of control.

Moms are great at solving all kinds of problems for their kids, but fathers think differently and have an essential perspective that kids need. My dad solved my angry tantrum problem in minutes while my mom couldn't solve it in years. And to be fair to my mom, she was far more present in my childhood than my dad, who was constantly at work, but he would insert himself at pivotal times like those. And that matters.

I took this lesson from my father and applied it to my own journey as a parent. Years ago, my son John Lucas started refusing to eat his dinner. I'd watch my wife beg, bargain, and even punish him for not eating, but nothing seemed to ease our stressful dining times. I wanted to help, but my wife shrugged off my advice as terrible and kept on with her own counsel. What was my advice? Simple! Don't make him eat dinner. Send him to bed hungry.

Finally, Rebekah, her compassion exhausted, gave up and handed the problem off to me. I looked at my son, dismissed him from the dinner table and told him to go straight to bed. He was shocked but cautiously got up from the table and started making his way upstairs. As he ascended the staircase, I announced, "This dinner will be waiting for you tomorrow morning for breakfast. If you do not eat it then, you can skip breakfast, and it will be waiting for you at lunch. You do not have to eat, but when you decide to, it will be this meal."

My wife did not like this strategy at all, but she was forced to admit that I was onto something she didn't understand when later that night I checked on my son and he let me know he was ready to eat. I brought him his cold dinner and watched him sit in bed, eating it with a smile on his face and a few fresh tears on his cheeks. The problem was solved, and it took me only one night of trying what I already knew was the answer. That's the power of a father in the life of a child.

Mothers are incredibly important in the development of a child. Without them, we wouldn't have kids at all! But moms do not always know best. There are some things men know better, and if Mom always gets her way, she's going to unintentionally turn a boy into a weak, entitled, little brat. It is through the mother's impulse to nurture the children and the father's instinct to make them strong that a child will grow up best. Parenting, at its best, consists of both a man and a woman bringing their strengths together for the benefit of the child.

SPIRITUAL NEEDS

We also need to develop our kids spiritually, which is the third leg of the table. Whatever your religion or philosophy, having a belief system that transcends your immediate needs and wants is a way of grounding you in a deeper reality.

As you should know by now, I am a very outspoken Christian. That's just how I roll, but I am respectful toward any creed so long as love and service to others are core tenets. In my mind, that's what makes a Warrior Poet. The spiritual dimension is where morality flows from; it's where we get our definition of "goodness." This is also where we find love and compassion, as well as connection and belonging.

Our spirituality is where we get a sense of fairness and wisdom, as well. You might think wisdom is mental, but to be truly wise is a spiritual pursuit. Certainly, there are many smart people with extensive knowledge about all kinds of things, but being able to apply that knowledge with restraint and temperance is something that flows from the core of who you are—from your spirit. It is something different from what happens between your ears. It's the moral fiber and character of your heart.

Wisdom comes from the soul, and we have to teach our children to be wise and good. We do this by modeling virtuous behavior, to be sure, but we also teach them through our humility, by apologizing when we miss the mark. Furthermore, we instruct our kids about right and wrong by giving them consequences for their actions and showing them what justice looks like. You don't get away with hurting other people in the real world, so why should you in the home? A good dad kindly but firmly teaches his kids these lessons, and they are profoundly spiritual.

MENTAL NEEDS

The final area of successful parenting is mental. We must teach our children to discipline and develop their minds. Critical thinking, creative problem-solving, memorization of important facts, and asking good questions to get true answers are all part of mental development.

Kids need to understand the laws of logic and be guided to a practical philosophy of how to go about life. One way we can do this is by nurturing a love for reading. When it comes to educating a child's mind, if you have helped them fall in love with reading, then you have done an amazing job. Certainly, there is more to helping children grow mentally than that, but reading is so underrated and a wonderful discipline that will reap a bounty of rewards for any person the rest of their life.

Your job as a parent is to be in charge of your child's education; that's not the job of a teacher or a school or even the government. It's up to you. How and what they learn will inform their worldview, so you better know what's going into that mind; because whatever goes in will eventually come out.

If we continue to follow the metaphor that your child is like a table, then we want to build sturdy legs all the way around so they don't wobble or fall down. To raise the best kids possible, we have to become the best dads we can. The more I grow as a father, the more I realize parenthood requires me to become a better man. It's a good challenge that, if you don't shy away from it or try to hide from the areas that threaten your ego, will leave you better than you were when you started.

As a dad, I'm constantly being stretched by my own inadequacies and failures, which are in my face each time I attempt to parent my children. I have a picture of the dad I want to be, and every step in this journey reveals where I'm falling short. It's not fun to face my shortcomings, but they keep teaching me that I can always be better. And so can you. Our kids deserve it.

MORE THAN PROVIDERS

Any dude who has ever become a parent has no idea what he's doing, at least not at first. When my firstborn came out of the womb, I thought he was dead. He was a sort of grayish purple, and no one warned me that babies come out purple. If you don't have kids yet, just know that; it's important.

They also come out with torpedo-like coneheads. Perhaps it's God's way of launching them into the world, I don't know. Anyway, when my boy was born, he had a weak cry, and I wasn't ready for that, either. In my mind, this thing was already over. My first thought was, "Well, that kid's dead," and I imme-diately shifted into comfort-the-spouse mode. Really.

In spite of my ignorance, my wife, with a marvel of maternal instincts, brought the baby to her chest and immediately bonded with him. He was just fine. I had no idea what to expect, but she knew; and he was *perfect*. The whole experience was wonderful, and it felt completely foreign. I had no idea what to do with a baby, but she did. All I knew was that I loved that baby boy and recognized there was something special between my wife and newborn son; an immediate bond formed between them.

I saw they had their own little world, the two of them, and this was a unique connection I got to be a part of at first. The same was true for our second child. It was a wonder to watch

Rebekah raise these little ones from babies to boys. But as they got older, they started shifting from mama's boys to becoming more interested in what Dad had to think and say. For our youngest, it started when we cut his little blond curls at age three so that he'd look more like a boy. Then it grew into wrestling and fighting and going on adventures together.

This is a shift that must happen for every son and father. The best way to raise a young man is to let another man lead their transition. Men make men; women make women. But whether you have girls or boys, they need a mother *and* a father. That's just how it works and always has. There are certain advantages each sex has over the other. That's why we're different! We bring unique gifts to the table, and it's silly to pretend otherwise.

Right now, we have this backward in society. In the famous words of Tyler Durden from the movie *Fight Club*, "We're a generation of men raised by women." More and more in this backward age of hyperfeminism and man-hating, we have mothers deciding how boys will be, even *what* boys will be, and it's no wonder we have a world full of men who are scared of their own masculinity and angry at everything. That's just not how it was meant to be.

Being a boy is confusing enough without having a woman try to tell you what it means to be one! And in all fairness, lest I sound like a misogynist, I couldn't raise a woman very well if I tried. I've never been a woman a single day of my life and don't intend to start anytime soon! But just as my wife has much to offer my sons, I do have much to offer a daughter. Consider the fact that teenage girls have a much higher chance of becoming pregnant when they are raised in fatherless homes.* A father leaves an indelible mark on the life of a child.

Fathers matter. Whether your dad was around a lot or not at all, he likely left a long-term mark on your soul. Maybe even the thought of that brings up unimaginable pain, joy, or a mixture of feelings. Regardless, we can't underestimate the effect men have on growing boys. You are still healing from the scars that were left or trying to pass on the gifts you received. Maybe both. Nonetheless, we cannot aspire to make the world a better place if we don't start with our youth. Fighting for the future means becoming better men ourselves so that we can raise the boys who will one day lead our world. We've got to let little children be poets so that they can eventually become the warriors we need them to be.

------

* Source: Rachel Nowak, "Absent Fathers Linked to Teenage Pregnancies," *New Scientist*, May, 15, 2003, newscientist.com/article/dn3724-absent-fathers -linked-to-teenage-pregnancies.

PRACTICUM

My kids call it "Daddy time," and it is a set period where they can do whatever they want and I'll join in. Oftentimes, it's just me saying, "I've got one hour, boys. . . . What do you want to do?"

This allows us to have intentional and distraction-free quality time. One hour of this kind of activity is worth more than five hours of just "hanging out."

If your kids are older and have more mature interests, you'll likely drop the title of "Daddy time" and just join in on whatever they're doing.

Regardless, your homework is to have some Daddy time with your kids. Let them pick, fully engage in whatever the activity is, and see their eyes and spirits light up as you give them the attention they deserve.

10

How to Stay Free

I prefer dangerous freedom over peaceful slavery.

—THOMAS JEFFERSON

T here are many ways to be free, and freedom is what every Warrior Poet fights for. To protect the liberties we all care about, we have to be strong in body, mind, and spirit, which is why we train so hard and often.

Discipline creates freedom, not just physically but spiritually and emotionally. We focus our minds and hearts so that we can be free from addiction, pain, and ignorance. Spiritual, emotional, and mental freedom are all essential to living life as a whole man. But without physical freedom, we may lack the luxury to even pursue other liberties.

There are two essential duties to a free man. The first is to safeguard freedom, and the second is to enjoy it. The second is just as important but is often neglected by those who fight for our hard-won liberties. As Samuel Johnson wrote, "To be happy at home is the ultimate result of all ambition, the end to which every enterprise and labor tends, and of which every desire prompts the prosecution."

You must use your gift of freedom to build a life that honors the "war" it took to get there, even if you never went to physical battle. Every man makes sacrifices to create a life for himself and the ones he loves. Remember to appreciate the gift of what you built and use it to make a positive impact on the lives around you and beyond. Use your freedom, and do not squander it on a meaningless life.

As we've already established, freedom is not native to the world. There are wolves hiding in plain sight, and others disguising themselves as good guys. Be on guard. Those who love freedom must be ready to defend it. But it is not enough to merely fight. To be the Warrior without the Poet is to live half a life. We must find ways to participate in the world we helped build and become free in all ways, both inside and out.

Fighting makes freedom possible, of course, and freedom makes fighting worthwhile—they power and rely on each other. We can't lose our warrior spirit, because a good society depends on man's willingness to go to battle. This same man, though, needs something to come home to: a life that makes the struggle worth the scars. A soldier whose relationships deteriorate will lose his will to fight and won't be able to fight anymore. We need to integrate into society in a way that still takes a stand for freedom.

After I left military life, I went back to college and entered the workplace. I noticed quickly how businesses and organizations adopted the language of "everyone working toward a common goal," but rarely did they mean it. At least, not in the way soldiers mean it. In corporate culture, it is every man for himself while the higher-ups co-opt the language of "teamwork."

War veterans go work for these businesses only to discover after several years of slugging it out "for the team" that the company is doing well, but no one was looking out for anyone but themselves. I have felt duped in the past by "team talk" that was really only a cheap facade for "our shareholders want higher profits." In the environment I'm thinking of, it was every man for himself, and I seemed to be the last to know it.

This can be quite disillusioning for someone who really is ready to sacrifice all for the cause. As a result, many soldiers are left in the dust, casualties of a system that didn't give back to them in any degree commensurate with what they contributed. It's a different world, and they don't know how to adapt. If you come from a military background, you are going to have to look out for your interests because "the company" almost always cares only about "the company." And "the company" doesn't include you, typically.

On the battlefield, it's pretty simple: you work hard, give your all to the mission, and the team takes care of you. We all take care of one another, in fact; our very lives depend on it. But it doesn't work the same way in the civilian world. They're not just going to hand you a career path on a silver platter; you have to fight for what is yours, and most soldiers aren't prepared for this.

Again, we seek balance. You must bring something of the Poet to the battlefield and something of the Warrior back home. That is, even in civilian life, you have to fight for freedom in everyday ways. For the rest of this chapter, I'll share with you practical tips and resources on how to maximize your liberties at home and how to become a more self-reliant man so that you can take care of yourself and others well.

BECOMING SELF-SUFFICIENT . . . AGAIN

Europeans in the eighteenth century seeking freedom from British tyranny fled across the Atlantic Ocean in droves to settle in North America. What they were looking for was a little patch of earth to call their own.

They wanted to build a home, plant some crops, have some kids, and be left alone from those who sought to control and exploit them. Freedom didn't just mean the opportunity to do what you wanted; it was, to them, the right to be left alone to live as they pleased.

Classically, a home was considered less a presentation of one's social status and thought more of as a pragmatic means of survival. The home was meant to be a refuge from the world. It was set up to self-sustain a family against cold winters, starvation, wild animals, and marauders. There was no power grid to plug into and no grocery stores down the street. A family lived surrounded by their livestock and crops. They cut firewood and seasoned it for cooking and heat. Your vocation may have supplemented your ability to stay alive, but your homestead was the real way you endured.

The last vestige of independence is the home. This is your territory, and it deserves to be fought for, maintained, and protected. It needs to be a safe place that is welcoming to all members of your family, including yourself. But like any liberty, it requires a warrior spirit lest it fall victim to the forces of chaos and attack.

We've spent significant time in this book exploring the necessity of being warriors, romancing women, and raising children well, but we haven't gotten into the brass tacks of what it takes to remain free. Freedom, as our forefathers understood it, was to be able to exist apart from a powerful ruler, warlord, or government. Freedom meant self-sufficiency.

Self-sufficiency is the act of not relying on any government, institution, or organization to take care of you. It means that you can provide for your family's basic needs without being dependent on a supply source controlled by someone else. While this was a common reality upon the early American frontier, nowadays in our era of grocery stores, Amazon deliveries, and power plants, self-sufficient people are as rare as unicorns.

In recent years, we've run into supply chain issues and various manufacturing crises. With the increase in inflation, rising prices for basic goods, and after seeing two years of lockdowns because of COVID-19, there has never been a better time to learn to live more self-sufficiently. Taking care of yourself and providing for your basic needs is an essential part of the masculine journey; it's an opportunity to become a better provider, too, because you have insulated yourself against all kinds of socioeconomic crises that may arise.

I don't know what'll happen in the near future, but I don't want to be caught on my heels when it does. I want to be able to make sure I can protect and provide for my family as best as I can. No one is able to predict what's coming, but we can prepare in the event that things continue to go sideways.

I'd rather plan for catastrophe and experience a slight bump in the road than the alternative. This is why we train, as men: to remind us that we ought to be ready at any moment for the unexpected. We can't anticipate every possible scenario, but we can stay vigilant and strong, ready for whatever fight decides to come knocking on our door.

Think of it in terms of the odds. Preparing for "the end of the world as we know it"—or at least a significant shift in modern society—is yet another way to train. I know this sounds a little doomsday-ish to some, but I'd rather be ready and have nothing happen than be devastated by the unexpected.

If you're prepared for the zombie apocalypse and no "walkers" come to eat your family, then you'll just end up with a bunch of canned beans and some really cool guns. (By the way, get silencers for your guns so that when the zombies do come, they aren't attracted to the sound of you offing one of their number. You're welcome for that little tip.)

Self-sufficiency is at the heart of what it means to be free. You have to be able to rely on yourself; otherwise you are a slave to society. And that begins with how well you can protect your home.

The prepared man doesn't freak out when crap hits the fan, because he planned for this as best he could. (He's also packing, so it's all good.) It might not go down exactly the way he thought, but if he's wise, he'll have thought of a few possible scenarios and done his best to anticipate each one and have a course of action ready to go.

Again, if nothing cataclysmic comes, you won't regret being a little more independent. Preparation is an antidote for fear. Some folks accuse the person who is moving toward self-sufficiency as being paranoid. But I've found the more prepared I am, the less trepidation I have for the future.

The naysayer is often the fearful one, because they cannot stand to even entertain the thought of bad times ahead. That's why they castigate your growing independence. It's because they know they aren't prepared and can't handle the thought of your being right. So whether you think the end is nigh or not, these are good things to do for anyone who wants to maximize their personal freedom. A massive added benefit is that it will help you spend less time in front of a screen and more time outside, and your kids will have plenty of chores so they learn to be self-sufficient, too.

What would you do if the grocery stores ran out of food? It's happened already multiple times in the United States in recent years and will probably happen again soon. What if the gas pumps aren't replenished? What if your power is cut off? Or maybe a lack of liberty will come from your boss, telling you to violate your convictions as a condition to keep your job. How would you feed your family? It'd be tough, I imagine. But imagine if you grew your own food and already had those basic necessities at your disposal.

So long as people are dependent on a system, they can be bullied by that system into complying. If a system provides you with all the things you need to survive, then that same system has the power to take away what you need to survive. In other words, if you are not self-sufficient, you are only as free as others decide you are.

DON'T BE VULNERABLE

What do we do to be ready for the worst possible scenario? Do we have to live in bunkers, wearing tinfoil hats? Are there ways we can become more self-sufficient that don't require us to look like loonies? Well, crazy is in the eye of the beholder, but I would argue there are simple steps any man can take to become more independent; and if the fabric of civilization comes apart, you'll be glad you did these things. If not, you'll be in a position where you won't be so dependent on others to survive, so it's a no-lose scenario.

The first step is to not be so vulnerable. This is relatively easy, but most people haven't taken the necessary measures. If you'd like to start making some steps toward self-sufficiency, you should begin by finding a way to stock emergency storage food and a lot of water.

If you can't feed your family, you're very easy to manipulate, intimidate, and control. Because what wouldn't you do to keep your family from starving? A fantastic stopgap is to have a month's worth of storage food on hand so that you and your family can stay free and healthy. That won't hold you forever, but it's a good place to start. If you've already stored a few months' worth of food, your next goal is a year.

There is storage food you can buy that is sealed and guaranteed to last more than twenty-five years, so there's no reason not to get started today. A bag of rice, beans, and some flour and sugar stays good for years and costs maybe a few bucks. Just do something. Start small and buy over time. I've been doing this for eight years now, and it's added up to quite a bit.

After food, the next one is obvious. *Guns.* Lots of guns.

If you are picturing the scene in *The Matrix* where Neo says that line and immediately sees shelves and shelves of awesome weaponry sail in all around him, then that's the right idea. Why do I want this? Because I'm a flesh-and-blood American male, that's why! Give me Neo's gun room; I want it!

In all seriousness, I do believe guns and ammo are important things to stock up on for a few reasons. First, they hold their value very well, which is important in a time of inflation and falling confidence in the dollar; second, you can use them for defense; and third, you can hunt and feed your family with them.

Furthermore, you never know what anti-gun legislation will prohibit your future access to guns and ammo, so ideally you should just go ahead and stockpile all the ammo you and your family will ever want or need. Easier said than done, I know, but we all need goals. Do what you can to start stocking up, because it won't hurt.

Before going after a ton of different guns, though, start with just a few and get tens of thousands of rounds. A gun is no good if it doesn't shoot anything. Having a million guns won't help you if you don't have anyone to shoot them with you. Focus on ammo and having a few friends nearby who can come to your aid, if you need it, and vice versa.

For decades now, politicians have been trying to regulate away our Second Amendment right to keep and bear arms. Their anti-constitutional attack has been to erode your rights via death by a thousand cuts. Some of these cuts are so old we don't even question them anymore.

The next thing to stock up on are standard weekly necessities. These are things like toilet paper, diapers, toothpaste, soap, rags, and so on. Think of it like preparing for a big storm that's coming through that might knock out your power for a few days. This sort of thing happens more often than your average apocalypse, so it makes sense to prepare for this first. You can worry about zombies after you have enough TP.

After that, make sure you get enough batteries in various sizes to help you power items like flashlights and essential electronics. Then, make sure you have enough fuel. This means gasoline, diesel (if you need it), smaller propane tanks for outdoor camping stoves, and plenty of wood for burning. Fuel is tricky to store long term, so don't get too crazy. Right now, I've got limited amounts of gasoline and diesel on hand and try to cycle them out, because they last only six to twelve months, depending on what's in them.

That said, fuel prices almost always increase over time, so you'll get more for your money today than you would tomorrow. Make sure you have plenty of fuel on hand for your vehicles. In case of a crisis, you don't want to be unable to get around. Fuels like propane last many years, and extra points if you can get your home on solar.

After that is alternate transportation. Recently, the used bike market went through the roof. At a time when gasoline is hard to get and quite costly, having a bunch of bicycles on hand could be a hedge against fossil fuels. I recently purchased some horses, since we live out in the country, and each one of them comes fully stocked with one whole horsepower—because, you know, it's a horse. I'd also like my transportation to run on grass instead of my legs. So that's a win-win.

Next on the list are survival gear items and basic tools. Ensure you have things to bushcraft or build with. In the tools category, make sure you have things such as hammers, saws, axes, crowbars, wrenches, and so on—plus a ton of screws and nails. Even if you live in an apartment or a rental, you'll want a decent tool kit in case the maintenance man is suddenly out of a job or bitten by a nuclear rabbit. Plus, any self-respecting dude should be able to fix something that breaks at home or at least have the tools to figure it out. I'm not saying you've got to become Tim "The Tool Man" Taylor. Just be ready to provide for your most basic needs in the event that it becomes necessary.

Next up are emergency medical equipment and medications such as acetaminophen, ibuprofen, anti-diarrhea, allergy medication, and any prescription drugs. Vitamins, too. Life is way harder and more annoying when you have a headache that won't go away, or you've got a nutrient deficiency that you can't treat.

After that, stock up on condiments and core ingredients for making food. This includes salt, ketchup, mayo, butter, and other basic seasonings. It's not enough to just have the basics. Say, hypothetically speaking, that you have a bunch of meat and no way to make it taste good. Well, my friend, you will die. Frozen meat is boring and tasteless without a little salt and butter. And don't forget the spicy mustard. (Sidebar: If you believe regular mustard is better than spicy mustard, please stop reading this book and rethink your life. Spicy is clearly better and all other opinions are wrong.)

Last (but not least) on the list are what I call "happy drinks." This means alcohol and coffee—so you don't die of low morale. I'm not kidding. Alcohol has all kinds of different and valuable uses, especially if things go sideways. At the very least it's a valuable barter item. Even if you don't drink (and I drink seldomly and only in moderation), make sure you have basic spirits like vodka and gin on hand. These can be used as disinfectants and to sterilize something, just like you've seen in the movies when a hero gets an arrow in his arm and needs to take a swig before lacerating the wound. You know what I'm talking about. Trust me, you'll need alcohol for that arrow as well as a couple of buddies to tear it out. And coffee, because duh, you want to be awake for the End.

All jokes aside, preparing for a few hard months is part of providing for the basic needs of your family. Whatever is important to you, stuff that you'll need in the near future, try to buy more today than you'll need, especially stuff that can "keep" for a long time and be easily stored. This list is by no means exhaustive, but it should be enough to start your wheels turning and get you on your way. Again, the goal is not to emergency-proof your life, per se, but to be more prepared than the average person for all kinds of potentially unfortunate events. Most people don't even do that, so you'll already be at an advantage if you do—which will only make you more self-sufficient.

BECOMING TYRANNY-PROOF

As I mentioned, I don't need to be paranoid—*because* I'm prepared. Preparation can be a glorious mitigator to paranoia. Fear is sitting around, worrying about what might happen. I don't do that, and many of the men I know who are stockpiling ammunition and food aren't doing that, either. We're not scared, because we're ready. The man with a boat isn't as afraid of drowning as the man treading water. Just like I'm not very fearful of an active shooter killing me or my family because, well, I'm armed and better trained than they are. Preparation trumps paranoia.

Many Americans live as if their current reality is all there has ever been or ever will be. But things are always changing, and never in the history of the world is there a long-standing age of peace and comfort. Even in American history we've seen world wars, a depression, natural disasters, and violent attacks. It would be naive to assume this state of things can and will last. To think that the good times will keep on going is naive and stupid.

Maybe this all sounds ludicrous, and maybe it is to some; but that's not my concern. As a Warrior Poet, my primary interest is freedom. One of the chief aims of my life is to find freedom at every level of existence. I want freedom from corrupt politicians and radical governments, from sin, from negative thinking and ignorance. I want freedom from bankruptcy and debt as well as any other form of financial need. I want to be as in control of my life as I can be. As Franklin D. Roosevelt said, "True individual freedom cannot exist without economic security and independence. People who are hungry and out of a job are the stuff of which dictatorships are made."

True independence must be fought for, protected, and stewarded. It is meant to be shared and spread. But if I am so dependent that I cannot even take care of myself, and the welfare state crushes our economy, turning us all into state-sponsored vassals, then I'm left to fight just to survive. I'm not much good to anyone at that point and certainly hindered in being able to wage war for the independence of others. If leaving to fight means your family will starve when you go, you won't go.

It is a rare thing to have long-lasting liberty. Rulers always want more, and the only thing that stands in their way is freedom-loving citizens like you and me who are brave enough to say no. Staying a free man, then, is not only your right; it is your responsibility.

You want to ensure a better life for your children and grand-children? You want to leave the world better than you found it? Learn to love freedom. Fight for it, first in your own life, then in the lives of others. Become as independent as you possibly can be. Don't rely too heavily on anyone; instead, do your best to be-come self-sufficient so that you can experience the luxury and blessing of being able to take care of others. We live in an in-credible age of opportunity when men in the free world can create an amazing life for themselves and their loved ones. Don't waste this chance to build something great. This window won't last for-ever, and the freedoms we love are already slowly being taken away.

We've got to be careful now. The fight is coming into our homes, on our laptops and screens and broadcast through the air. It's sneaking into the lives of our children and spouses and friends. Today, we fight in an ideological war that threatens to derail our very system of liberty. Many people get their power now by offering the feeling of democracy while secretly stacking the deck against it.

For instance, to carry a gun you have to get a permit *from the government*. Think about that. You have to get permission from the state to exercise your right that exists to protect you from the state. We must get permission from the government to be able to have the ability to resist the government. That's crazy. In other countries, the citizens have no right to defend themselves against potential government corruption, hostile neighbors, and so on. Many laws infringe upon our most basic rights to self-protection, and we just take it. I call that tyranny.

To be free, we have to be able to protect ourselves from a lack of freedom. If I want to know how free a country is, I look at that nation's laws regarding gun ownership. If the government heavily regulates or deems guns illegal, then they are not free enough. In an instant, the government can away all other freedoms and the people have no recourse. The right to bear arms is the freedom that protects all other freedoms, because it keeps humans somewhat safe from the powers of force and coercion. Without it, we are all more vulnerable to attack, especially from our own government.

Look at what happened in Australia, with the tyranny that occurred during the COVID lockdowns in 2020 and beyond. The United States was overzealous in some aspects of its response but nothing like what happened in some of the major Australian cities like Sydney, where people were forced to stay at home for weeks on end and entire economies basically shut down. Why the discrepancy in response? Perhaps, in part, because many Americans have guns and will only stand for so much.

The first steps to staying free, then, are having the means to feed and protect ourselves. Otherwise, we are weaker than we realize, one small step away from losing everything. That's not a level of vulnerability I am comfortable with, and I hope you aren't, either. Whatever you can do to gird yourself against potential attacks from those who claim to govern you is a wise choice.

This is what every tyrant tries to do: take the people's guns, control their speech and ideas through the media, and reprogram the nation's youth. The details of how this is done vary over time, but the plan is invariably the same. When tyranny has come to roost, dissenters will be jailed or shipped off to work camps. For those of us who love liberty, we have to be watchful, to be aware of what is happening, and do everything we can to protect ourselves.

The best way to become tyranny-proof is to need very little from your fellow man. Our greatest defense against injustice is to be as free as we possibly can. Just like America's Founding Fathers intended, we must be willing to speak up against all kinds of hostile forces and be prepared to defend ourselves and our ideals from those who might try to take them away.

Cowardice can be contagious, but so is courage. If you and I speak courageously to each other long enough, we all become braver. When our connection to each other is severed, we are left alone and vulnerable to forces of intimidation. Everything we love rides on our willingness to protect the liberties we take for granted and band together. Because one day, you're going to need this freedom far more than you imagined.

The voices of modern-day tyranny may try to bury you, cancel you, even discredit you, but the man who speaks up for what's right inspires others to do the same. This is how we remember we are not alone. We keep saying what must be said and taking the stands that must be taken.

In the famous words of Winston Churchill: "Never give in, never give in, never, never, never, never—in nothing, great or small, large or petty—never give in except to convictions of honor and good sense. Never yield to force; never yield to the apparently overwhelming might of the enemy."

PRACTICUM

Are you plugged into external institutions of power for your daily survival?

Do you have any money on hand or is it all in the bank?

Do you have any storage food, or are you dependent on the grocery store each week?

Take a step to become more self-reliant and free today. The goal is not total independence tomorrow. That's impossible. But the more you depend on others for your survival, the more vulnerable you are.

We all can be making greater strides toward becoming tyranny-proof.

Which reminds me: I need to go fill up my gas tanks.

CONCLUSION

LIVE FREE, DIE WELL

While I thought that I was learning how to live, I have been learning how to die.

—LEONARDO DA VINCI

L et's wrap up where we all end up: six feet underground. If we are going to die, what does it mean to really live? Most men go to the grave pursuing pointless pleasures that ultimately disappoint. They live incomplete and desperate lives, never measuring up to their potential and dying in vain.

To die well, you need to live well, which means you need something worth fighting for, a cause to believe in with such conviction that you are willing to not only stand up and defend it but lay down your very life for it. A life of significance will end in a death of significance. So, how *do* you live well?

You become a Warrior Poet, discovering that warrior spirit buried in the recesses of your soul. You face the coward within and become a dangerous man. In humility, you realize how far you have to go and all the areas of weakness you still have to work through.

You live as if you were dying, aware that death is always around the corner, never taking it for granted. You wield truth as a weapon in defense of what is right and good, speaking up in the face of evil, disciplining your mind to always be learning and growing. You pursue your muse daily with passion and gusto, dancing with her—and all of life—as you go.

You commit to chipping off the sharp edges of you, so that you can love and lead better. You chase goodness above any thought of greatness, keeping eternity in your sights at all times, remembering that your legacy is being written in real time, happening in this very moment.

And even though it's difficult, you keep your priorities straight, making room in life for loved ones. You stay humble and apologize when you spend your time in stupid, foolish ways.

Not least of all, you never forget that freedom is not just given; it is also taken. The world is dangerous, and you must always be ready for a fight—and always ready to enjoy the freedom you fought so hard for.

In this book, I've shared with you these principles and this ideal of what a whole man ought to be. But really, if I'm being honest, what I am describing is *my* ideal: the only man who has ever lived perfectly. A man so noble and good, so powerful and humble, that all of human history is divided around His thirty-three years of life on this Earth.

His birth now splits time in two, and His little hometown of Bethlehem stands in our geographic center of the world. This man did not walk among us long, but He lived well: in the service of others, pursuing the highest ideal, and humbling Himself to the point of death. He is the most famous man to have ever lived, died—and then, if you believe what I believe, lived again.

Wherever you are on the spectrum of belief is your business, but I would be remiss if I did not pull back the curtain entirely and share where I'm coming from. Because you can get pretty close to the world's standard of "good" and still fall completely short. This is why having an ideal that is not only greater than what I can do but gives me the very picture of goodness is not only helpful—it is absolutely necessary. In life, everything hangs on what you aim at.

EMBRACING A LARGER STORY

Just this morning, I sat alone by my kitchen window, sipping coffee and reflecting on my life while working on this book. It was still dark outside, and my family had not yet stirred. Thinking to myself, I heard a voice in my head ask, *Am I living a bigger story? Or has the rat race once again sucked me in?*

I wasn't sure my answer was no, and that frightened me. You see, even in listing out all these wonderful ideas and principles, I know how wicked and twisted I can sometimes be. I know how selfish and cold I get, how easily something can upset me. I know what darkness lurks in my heart, and I am aware of how bad I can be if my steps are not inspired, directed, and disciplined. In light of history, I am forced to consider my little story in the greater narrative of all creation.

As a warrior, I am inclined to look back at the men who came before me, who walked this same path and dealt with these same struggles. The great freedom fighters of old, I believe, saw themselves wrapped up in a larger story than what their lives could contain. This is why they were willing to die for such a mission. They fought against oppression, waged war on the forces of tyranny and evil, put their very lives on the line for the well-being of their families and countrymen. They sacrificed themselves for a cause greater than themselves, and their example challenges me to this day.

Am I doing the same? I am not so sure.

It's not enough to live a comfortable life, to work hard and protect your family, to treat your kids to vacations and your wife to dates. It is not sufficient to merely become a strong man, capable of violence and self-control, who is skilled at fighting. It's not even enough to have a noble purpose you are willing to die for. Even the psychopath or terrorist can do that. These things can be good, but in themselves, they are not necessarily good enough reasons to sacrifice your life for.

Great men of old understood something that many of us miss in modern times: they saw themselves as actors in an epic narrative. They could see a grand play before them, and they were clear on their own role in it. This is the difference between significance and insignificance. You have to have a good reason to willingly die, which means you have been living for something larger than yourself.

So I must turn the question to you: *Are you living a bigger story?*

Do you and I share anything in common with the great men who came before us? If not, we have work to do. My hunch about these men is they didn't want the legacies many modern people now ascribe to them. They weren't seeking adoration or accolades or any of that. These men, by and large, were after something better.

My greatest hero turned down opportunities to become an influential political leader. He deflected his followers' attempts to wage war on his people's oppressors. He did just about everything the opposite of what we think a "great man" would do today, and he changed history.

So, this morning, as I sat here contemplating my own legacy, I thought to myself: *I'm not great. Not even close.* One day, I hope to be *good* enough to not even have to consider such a question. But for now, I'm still pressing toward the ideal set by so many who came before—because of one who set an impossible standard.

Nonetheless, it is my greatest privilege to be counted among other like-minded warriors who are committed to working on themselves and striving to create a better world for themselves and their children. I know I have work to do, and there is more that I could be, so I keep striving. I also know that, with the right example, I am capable of getting better and being forgiven when I fall short. This gives me hope and courage.

You and I, whether we realize it or not, are caught up in a story greater than that of our own little lives. Our stories are part of this narrative but far from the whole thing. We are characters in an epic that predates even the birth of our ancestors. In my experience, it's not enough to trust this story. You have to surrender to it, which is the last thing a warrior wants.

But if you really want to live free and die well, that begins today, with letting go of your easy-to-control narrative and submitting to one so much more mysterious than you could ever imagine. When you do this, living for yourself is just plain boring. What a waste of life that would be! Instead, you are no longer concerned with your own glory or what they will say about you when you are gone. You don't worry about dying well, because you're living well.

As I sat at that table, what came to mind was a poem. And because this book began with a fight and the work of the Warrior, it made sense to end with a little poetry. Each word spoke to me specifically and with intention, so I wrote them all down:

> *We cannot hear the great story.*
> *It is fool's gold*
> *to live for self,*
> *It is a rotting grave—*
> *reaching.*
> *Locked in a house*
> *with mirrors for walls,*

we cannot see a burning son
risen.
We cannot hear the greatest story.
It is fool's gold
to live for self,
and the shine is quickly fading.

—JOHN LOVELL

Don't be fooled by the allure of living an easy, materialistic, but ultimately meaningless, life. Don't live for the imaginary prize at the end of the rainbow, limiting your life to vague notions of success. When you have a reason to die well, you'll discover an even better way to live. Your life takes on greater meaning and purpose and feels like an unpredictable adventure full of mystery and excitement.

When you discover the great story, the one into which you were born, the one that existed before even time began, you see what you must do, what your true mission is—and it has so very little to do with you that it's humbling to be able to play a part at all. You realize this has been waiting for you all the time, your whole life till now. That's grace. That's something worth living—and dying—for. That's the way of the Warrior Poet. Now, let's get on with it.

PRACTICUM

Give yourself a high five for finishing this book.

I'm serious! It's no small feat to work through something and complete it.

May you do the same with your life, committing yourself to the highest ideal and finishing with integrity and honor.

I hope you live for many years to come, but when you inevitably do meet your end, my wish is that you die as you lived: well.

ACKNOWLEDGMENTS

Thank you to Jesus, the author and perfecter of my faith. I am first and foremost who I am because He rescued me and put me on an entirely different path—one from death to life.

Thank you to my wife, Rebekah, for helping with this book over the course of a few years. She was a constant source of encouragement as well as a helpful hand in rewording, editing, and prompting me to include things that were missing but escaped my notice.

Thank you to my sons, John Lucas and Judah. You are on the path, and I am so proud to be your father. You have made an indelible mark on inspiring me to be a better man and dad.

Thanks to my fellow Warrior Poet peers out there, some of whom I've referenced in the book. Their living examples have made me better and is making me better still.

Thanks to Jeff Goins, who was instrumental in helping me arrange my thoughts and hammering into shape this book.

Thank you to my team at Penguin Random House for making this book happen: Helen Healey for helping me map out what this book could and should be, as well as Bria Sandford and Megan McCormack for working your editorial magic.

I also would not be who I am without my parents, who equipped me with wisdom and lifelong lessons, much of which can be found in this book. And to my wrestling coaches for helping me transition from boyhood to manhood. You taught me the most important stuff I learned in the totality of my time in high school.

To my brothers in the 75th Ranger regiment who walked through the fire with me and always watched my six. I'm alive today, and I'm made tougher and more courageous because of you.

VISIT THE WARRIOR POET SOCIETY WEBSITE

warriorpoetsociety.com